John W Simons

A Familiar Treatise on the Principles and Practice of Masonic

Jurisprudence

John W Simons

A Familiar Treatise on the Principles and Practice of Masonic Jurisprudence

ISBN/EAN: 9783337312336

Printed in Europe, USA, Canada, Australia, Japan

Cover: Foto ©Lupo / pixelio.de

More available books at **www.hansebooks.com**

Fraternally

John W. Simons

A

FAMILIAR TREATISE

ON THE

PRINCIPLES AND PRACTICE

OF

MASONIC JURISPRUDENCE.

BY

JOHN W. SIMONS,

PAST GRAND MASTER OF NEW YORK.

―――――

"*Stand on the Old Ways and then make Progression..*"—BACON.

―――――

NEW YORK:

MASONIC PUBLISHING AND MANUFACTURING CO.,

432 BROOME STREET.

1869.

PREFACE.

In presenting the following pages to the attention of the Fraternity, we are but repeating a thrice-told tale, and should, perhaps, apologize for attempting a topic which has already been so exhaustively treated by brethren learned in the law. Our title will, however, indicate our design, which is to bring the subject within the grasp of the Fraternity in general, and, by our method of treatment, to make it comprehensible to those who have heretofore deemed it too abstruse for the common intellect, and have therefore been satisfied to accept the decisions of any whom they might deem qualified to instruct them.

The lamentable want of knowledge, in regard to the simplest principles of Masonic law, which prevails even among otherwise intelligent brethren, can only be fully known to those who, like the writer, have held official station in the Craft, and been called upon to answer the multitudinous questions that arise in the practice of lodges. A dozen different interrogatories are frequently propounded in relation to the same subject, all of which might be readily answered, were the questioners in possession of the fundamental principle on which it is based. To supply this principle, and to simplify its application, has been the object in view in our work; and to it we have brought the experience of a long and active participation in every branch of our institution, with an extended intercourse with Craftsmen from every portion of our own country and Europe.

Our plan has been, as will be found upon examination of the work, to reduce the authorities depended upon to the smallest compass, and to make a careful distinction between the general laws of the society and the local regulations of Grand Lodges, which

we have found, in our practice, to be the principal source of difficulty among brethren unused to the application of the law to the
questions presenting themselves in their lodges.   Commencing
thus at the foundation, we have followed the profane from his petition onward to his reception in a lodge, and explained, in the fewest
words possible, the various rules and requirements that attend his
progress.   The formation of a lodge, and the powers thereof, as
well as the prerogatives of its officers and members, are considered.
The laws applicable to trials and appeals have received special
consideration; and thus the inquirer is led forward to the establishment of Grand Lodges, and the powers and prerogatives of
the Grand Officers.

We are by no means vain enough to suppose that we have
exhausted the questions at issue, or that nothing more is to be
said on the subject; but we do believe that the great number of
brethren unacquainted with the jurisprudence of the Fraternity
will find here useful hints to guide their progress in the study of
the laws which govern our institution, and to point out the paths
which lead to a correct understanding of the foundations upon
which our system of jurisprudence is based.

In the Appendix will be found the various forms required in the
business of lodges; among which, we desire to call especial attention to those regarding trials and appeals, which have been adopted
by the Grand Lodge of New York, and which we deem the best
that have yet been presented to the notice of the brethren.   Prepared originally by our friend and brother, the M. W. JOHN L.
LEWIS, they have proved in practice to be all that can be required
in the administration of Masonic justice.

And, in conclusion, we would say, that if our labors shall prove
to be of benefit to our brethren, and aid, even in a feeble degree,
in making the subject treated more comprehensible to them, we
shall feel amply compensated for the labor expended in its
preparation.

THE AUTHOR.

PRINCIPLES AND PRACTICE

OF

MASONIC JURISPRUDENCE.

CHAPTER I.

The Law.——Landmarks.

THE MASONIC INSTITUTION is complete in itself. Appointed, as we believe, an agent to assist in the development of the purposes of our creation and earthly existence, it moves silently forward in its mission, without resort to exterior agencies, and labors at its appointed task by methods of its own, and from designs drawn on its tracing-boards by no profane hand. Its history, its philosophy, its ethics, and its symbolism, each bear the signet of the Craft; each is a study in itself, that no single mind, however industrious its possessor, can be said to have yet completely mastered. So with its laws: they are a portion of the system, stamped with its peculiar im press, and only to be rightly comprehended when viewed in the light that belongs to the institution. Without a knowledge of the society—its rituals and

customs—the most learned judge, the most subtle
advocate, would be at a loss to declare the law on a
given point, or even to rightly interpret its written
code. It should not, therefore, be a matter of surprise
that, to the great majority of the brethren, this subject presents almost insuperable difficulties, and that
it is so rare to find one who has devoted the time and
investigation necessary to a proper comprehension
of it; they learn, it is true, the general routine of
lodge business with sufficient promptitude, but beyond
that, they rarely go; suffering themselves—as in the
ordinary affairs of life—to be guided by the few, and
accepting (perhaps in too many instances) the decisions of any one in whom they may place confidence.
We can, however, imagine no reason why the lay
brethren—to say nothing of Masters and other officers of lodges—should not understand this, as well
as other matters of Masonic peculiarity; and it is to
encourage and facilitate such inquiry that we have
undertaken the present work, devoted, as will be
found upon examination, rather to pointing out what
the law really is, than to inventing apologies for or
arguments against its provisions. The Masonic code,
though not so plain that a wayfaring man may not
err therein, is nevertheless not so intricate, nor is its
study so dry and forbidding as many suppose. Its
foundation rests upon three principles of action,

which are well and concisely stated in the following extract from the Constitution of the Grand Lodge of the State of New York:

" The action of Freemasons, in their Grand or Subordinate Lodges, or in their individual character, is regulated and controlled—

" 1. By ANCIENT LANDMARKS; or, the Unwritten Law of Masonry.

" 2. By WRITTEN CONSTITUTIONS and General Regulations; and,

" 3. By USAGES, CUSTOMS, RULES, EDICTS, and RESOLUTIONS, having the force of GENERAL REGULATIONS.

" The Ancient Landmarks are those principles of Masonic government and polity which are the only part of Masonic law, or rule of government, that may never be altered or disturbed; and such of them as are lawful to be written, are usually, but not wholly, engrafted in the written Constitutions and General Regulations.

" Constitutions are those written compacts or laws adopted by Freemasons for the government of a Grand Lodge and its Subordinate Lodges, and their members; including General Regulations, constitutionally adopted, that are intended to be permanent in their character.

" General Regulations, Usages and Customs, Rules, Edicts and Resolutions, are those Masonic rules of action adopted by competent authority for local or temporary purposes, admitting of change at convenience, and not embraced in Ancient Landmarks or Constitutions, and are frequently termed By-Laws. But when they so operate as to alter, modify, or otherwise affect the Constitutions, as defined in the preceding section, they are also styled Constitutions."

We remark, in passing, that the Landmarks are not all comprised in the unwritten law: on the contrary, some of the most important are found in the Ancient Charges and Regulations. Of the three principles above set forth, however, the Landmarks are undoubtedly the most important, being, as it were, the starting-point, and, from their very nature, influencing the formation and controlling the validity of the others. And yet they are the most difficult to be understood and defined. The term "*Landmark*" is used in its scriptural sense where it is employed to designate a mark or boundary set up in ancient days between one man's possessions and those of his neighbor, beyond which neither party could lawfully go; and, when once established, these boundaries or landmarks were never to be removed. This custom has come down to us unimpaired, it being a law in most, if not all the States, that a tree, stone, or other landmark, between the possessions of neighbors, cannot be cut down or removed. It is in this sense that we apply the word in Masonic law and usage, as designating a fundamental principle of Masonry, which no man or body of men can change or remove—as one on which we rely to preserve the institution from the changes of the outer world, and to hand it down to the latest posterity, as it was in the beginning, and must continue to be to the end of time. But, paradoxical as it may appear, that there should be any uncertainty about that which is, in its nature, fixed and unchangeable, it is nevertheless quite true that scarcely any two Masonic authorities of eminence agree as to what are, and what are not, Landmarks. We assume those principles of action to be landmarks which have existed from time immemorial, whether in the written or unwritten law; which are identified with the form and essence of the society; which, the great majority agree, cannot be changed, and which every Mason is bound to maintain intact, under the most solemn and inviolable sanctions. In accordance with these views, we think that the following will be admitted to have always been in force; to involve essential Masonic principles; to be unchangeable, unless by altering the form and essence of the institution, and therefore to be landmarks, in the proper sense of the term.

LANDMARKS.

1. A belief in the existence of a Supreme Being, and in the immortality of the soul.

2. That the moral law, which inculcates, among

other things, charity and probity, industry and sobriety, is the rule and guide of every Mason.

3. Respect for, and obedience to, the civil law of the country, and the Masonic regulations of the jurisdiction where a Mason may reside.

4. That new-made Masons must be free-born, of lawful age, and hale and sound at the time of making.

5. The modes of recognition, and, generally, the rites and ceremonies of the three degrees of Ancient Craft Masonry.

6. That no appeal can be taken to the Lodge, from the decision of the Master, or the Warden occupying the Chair in his absence.

7. That no one can be the Master of a Warranted Lodge till he has been installed and served one year as Warden.

8. That when a man becomes a Mason, he not only acquires membership in the particular lodge that admits him, but, in a general sense, he becomes one of the whole Masonic family; and hence he has a right to visit, masonically, every regular lodge, except when such visit is likely to disturb the harmony or interrupt the working of the lodge he proposes to visit.

9. The prerogative of the Grand Master to preside over every assembly of the Craft, within his jurisdiction, to make Masons at sight in a regular lodge,

and to grant Dispensations for the formation of new lodges.

10. That no one can be made a Mason, save in a regular lodge, duly convened, after petition, and acceptance by unanimous ballot, except when made at sight by the Grand Master.

11. That the ballot for candidates is strictly and inviolably secret.

12. That a lodge cannot try its Master.

13. That every Mason is amenable to the laws and regulations of the jurisdiction in which he resides, even though he be a member of a particular lodge in some other jurisdiction.

14. The right of the Craft at large to be represented in Grand Lodge, and to instruct their representatives.

15. The general aim and form of the society, as handed down to us by the fathers, to be by us preserved inviolate, and transmitted to our successors forever.

This list might be somewhat extended by adding to it, as is frequently done, regulations deduced from these principles; but we prefer to avoid that error, and the discussions which inevitably follow a departure from established law: for self-interest, or the predominance of a feeling entirely extraneous to

Masonry, will sometimes lead men to close their
eyes to the most indubitable proposition. Take, for
instance, the fourth landmark, above cited. Its existence, as a fundamental principle of Masonic law,
from the very earliest times of which we have any
record, is beyond dispute : its language is too plain
to admit of any equivocation ; and it is just as much
an integral and immovable part of the Masonic system, as the one requiring a belief in the existence of
a Supreme Being; and we can admit an argument
as to the right to abrogate one, with the same propriety as the other. Nevertheless, the Grand Lodge
of England, a few years since, solemnly amended its
Constitution by striking out "free-*born*," and putting
in its place "free-*man*;" thus changing an essential
feature of the law, or, in plain terms, removing an
indisputable landmark. We can easily perceive that
it would take but a few such alterations of the landmarks to destroy the identity of the society, and
sever the links that bind it to the long past. Admit
the power to modify these principles at the pleasure
of Grand Lodges, and you at once overturn the whole
structure; sever the present from the past as completely as if the past had never been ; bring to nought
the boasted antiquity of the Fraternity, and make its
most solemn covenants but empty words.

There is a double iniquity in this proceeding of the

English Grand Lodge, from the fact that, at its establishment, it was solemnly agreed that no regulation should be adopted in derogation of the Ancieut Landmarks, and that agreement is just as binding as a landmark; for it was entered into as a condition of the resignation of the general sovereignty into the keeping of the Grand Lodge, which, therefore, not only sets aside a landmark, but violates an express stipulation that it would not do so.

We could easily assign the reason for this proceeding, were any useful purpose to be subserved by so doing. It is sufficient for us to show, however, that the English Craft are themselves at a loss to justify their own acts, as will be seen by the following extract from a late English work :*

"The strict inviolability of a Landmark is somewhat problematical. There are certain obsolete particulars in Masonry which were formerly esteemed to be Landmarks, but have undergone alterations in a greater or lesser degree. It follows, therefore, that if the old Landmarks cannot, by any possibility, be removed, then we incur the unavoidable conclusion that these never had a claim to any such distinction. In all existing constitutions, however, there is a prohibitory clause, which pronounces the Landmarks, like the laws of the

* *The Freemason's Treasury.* Fifty-two short lectures on the theory and practice of symbolical Masonry, by the Rev. GEORGE OLIVER, D. D. London, 1863.

Medes and Persians, to be unchangeable; but we shall find that, in practice, it has been occasionally violated, and therefore inapplicable to all the contingencies that may arise in practice.

"To persist, then, in asserting that the Landmark cannot be altered, with an array of positive facts against the hypothesis, is indefensible and absurd, because it places the society in a false position. It is well known, that whenever it has been found expedient to expunge a Landmark, the means of accomplishment were never wanting. The letter of the law is stern, but the spirit is feeble. Practice is more than a match for it: it beats it on its own ground."

This is undoubtedly a fair exposition of English "practice," and goes to show the method that must have governed the Grand Lodge in the case before cited. They resolved—1, The regulation that a candidate must be free-born is obsolete; 2, It is not a landmark; and, 3, That it be rescinded. By this process of reasoning, it would be easy to prove the non-existence of any Landmark; and its natural consequence would be to gradually remove, not only the landmarks, but the society itself. We regret that so able an exponent of the Masonic ideal as Dr. OLIVER should be willing to countenance such proceedings; we wonder that, instead of so doing, he had not raised his voice in indignant remonstrance; and we sincerely trust that the day may never come when an American Mason will be found willing to countenance so manifest an innovation, however exalted may be the source from which it emanates; that all and singular will maintain the doctrine that any such action or attempted action, on the part of a Grand Lodge or other assembly of Masons, would be absolutely void and of no effect.

To resume : All Constitutions, General Regulations and Usages are based upon the Landmarks, and must be in harmony with them ; for otherwise they would have no binding force or effect.   But every Grand Lodge has an inherent right to make local regulations ; to abolish old ones, and to make new ones at pleasure ; but such regulations, it will be understood, will only be valid within the jurisdiction of the Grand Lodge promulgating them.   It is, however, a very common mistake among the brethren to confound such local regulations with the general laws of the fraternity, from which source emanate many of the questions submitted for the decision of Grand Masters and Grand Lodges.   The inquiring brother should, therefore, be acquainted with, and study for himself, the basis of the Masonic law, and the superstructure of Masonic jurisprudence that has been erected upon it.

Masonic jurists claim the authority of law for the Gothic or York Constitutions of A. D. 926; for various regulations adopted at subsequent periods, and for the Charges and Regulations compiled by Doctor

ANDERSON in 1721, and published under sanction of
the Grand Lodge of England in 1723. These Constitutions are claimed to have embodied all the regulations of the Craft up to that time, not only in
England, but of " Lodges beyond sea ;" and as they
certainly contain all the law of a general nature that
we have, we see no good reason for multiplying authorities, and our references will be made to them.
We are the more inclined to this opinion, from the
fact that they were collated immediately after the
revival in 1717, by one to whom every facility for
making them correct was extended, and before the
increase of the fraternity, under the new regime, led
to the innovations which appear in subsequent edi-
tions.   It should be observed, too, that during the
schism in England, LAWRENCE DERMOTT, who was
Deputy Grand Master of the seceding, or Athol
Grand Lodge, published a "Book of Constitutions,"
similar in its general features to the true version, but
in which he took occasion to make alterations in
some essential points, probably to suit the exigencies
of his irregular Grand Lodge.   Many of the warrants
for the establishment of lodges in this country issued
from the Dermott or Athol Grand Lodge, which is
doubtless the reason why so much of the spurious
Constitutions is found in the jurisprudence of the
several States.   In New York, where most of these

warrants were ultimately located, the spurious *Charges* of DERMOTT are prefixed to and made a part of the Book of Constitutions, and more or less of their spirit is found in its otherwise admirable code of law.

As a matter of research, the Regulations, previous to 1721, may be consulted; but, for all practical purposes, the Charges and Thirty-nine Articles of Doctor ANDERSON are sufficient. For this reason, and to avoid confusing the mind of the student, we insert these only.

The Charges of a Freemason.

Extracted from the Ancient Records of Lodges beyond Sea, and of those in England, Scotland and Ireland, for the use of the Lodges in London. To be read at the making of New Brethren, or when the Master shall order it.

THE GENERAL HEADS, *viz:*

I.—OF GOD and RELIGION; II.—Of the CIVIL MAGISTRATE, Supreme and Subordinate; III.—Of LODGES; IV.—Of MASTERS, WARDENS, FELLOWS, and APPRENTICES; V.—Of the Management of the CRAFT in working; VI.—Of BEHAVIOR, *viz:* 1. In the Lodge while CONSTITUTED. 2. After the Lodge is over, and the BRETHREN not gone. 3. When Brethren meet without STRANGERS, but not in a LODGE. 4. In presence of STRANGERS NOT MASONS. 5. At HOME and in the NEIGHBORHOOD. 6. Towards a STRANGE BROTHER.

I.—CONCERNING GOD AND RELIGION.

A Mason is obliged, by his tenure, to obey the moral law; and if he rightly understands the Art, he will never be a

stupid Atheist, nor an irreligious Libertine. But though in
ancient times Masons were charged in every country to be
of the Religion of that country or nation, whatever it was,
it is now thought more expedient only to oblige them to that
Religion in which all men agree, leaving their particular opinions to themselves; that is, to be *good men and true*, or men
of honor and honesty, by whatever denominations or persua-
sions they may be distinguished; whereby Masonry becomes
the **Center** of **Union**, and the means of conciliating true
Friendship among persons that must have remained at a
perpetual distance.

II.—OF THE CIVIL MAGISTRATE, SUPREME AND SUBORDINATE.

A Mason is a peaceable subject to the civil powers wherever he resides or works, and is never to be concerned in
plots and conspiracies against the peace and welfare of the
nation, nor to behave himself undutifully to inferior magistrates; for as Masonry hath been always injured by war,
bloodshed, and confusion, so ancient kings and princes have
been much disposed to encourage the Craftsmen, because of
their peaceableness and loyalty, whereby they practically
answered the cavils of their adversaries, and promoted the
honor of the Fraternity, who ever flourished in times of peace.
So that if a Brother should be a rebel against the State, he
is not to be countenanced in his rebellion, however he may be
pitied as an unhappy man; and, if convicted of no other
crime, though the loyal brotherhood must and ought to disown
his rebellion, and give no umbrage or ground of political jealousy to the government for the time being, they cannot expel
him from the lodge, and his relation to it remains indefeasible.

III.—OF LODGES.

A Lodge is a place where Masons assemble and work: Hence that Assembly, or duly organized Society of Masons, is called a *Lodge*, and every Brother ought to belong to one, and to be subject to its by-laws and the General Regulations. It is either particular or general, and will be best understood by attending it, and by the Regulations of the General or Grand Lodge hereunto annexed. In ancient times, no Master or Fellow could be absent from it, especially.when warned to appear at it, without incurring a severe censure, until it appeared to the Master and Wardens that pure necessity hindered him.

The persons admitted members of a lodge must be good and true men, free-born, and of mature and discreet age; no bondmen, no women, no immoral or scandalous men, but of good report.

IV.—OF MASTERS, WARDENS, FELLOWS AND APPRENTICES.

All preferment among Masons is grounded upon real worth and personal merit only; that so the lords may be well served, the brethren not put to shame, nor the Royal Craft despised: Therefore no Master or Warden is chosen by seniority, but for his merit. It is impossible to describe these things in writing, and every Brother must attend in his place, and learn them in a way peculiar to this Fraternity: Only candidates may know that no Master should take an Apprentice, unless he has sufficient employment for him, and unless he be a perfect youth, having no maim or defect in his body, that may render him incapable of learning the art of serving his master's LORD, and of being made a *Brother*, and then a *Fellow*

Craft in due time, even after he has served such a term of
years as the custom of the country directs; and that he should
be descended of honest parents; that so, when otherwise qualified, he may arrive to the honor of being the *Warden,* and
then the *Master* of the Lodge, the *Grand Warden,* and at
length the *Grand Master* of all the Lodges, according to
his merit.

No Brother can be a Warden until he has passed the part
of a Fellow Craft; nor a Master until he has acted as a
Warden, nor Grand Warden until he has been Master of a
Lodge, nor GRAND MASTER, unless he has been a Fellow Craft
before his election, who is also to be nobly born, or a gentle-
man of the best fashion, or some eminent scholar, or some
curious architect or other artist, descended of honest parents,
and who is of singular great merit in the opinion of the
lodges.   And for the better, and easier, and more honorable
discharge of his office, the **Grand Master** has a power to
choose his own Deputy Grand Master, who must be then, or
must have been formerly, the Master of a particular lodge,
and has the privilege of acting whatever the Grand Master,
his Principal, should act, unless the said Principal be present,
or interpose his authority by a letter.

These rulers and governors—supreme and subordinate—
of the ancient Lodge, are to be obeyed in their respective
stations by all the Brethren, according to the old Charges and
Regulations, with all humility, reverence, love and alacrity.

V.—OF THE MANAGEMENT OF THE CRAFT IN WORKING.

All Masons shall work honestly on working-days, that they
may live creditably on holy-days; and the time appointed

by the law of the land, or confirmed by custom, shall be observed.

The most expert of the Fellow Craftsmen shall be chosen or appointed the Master or Overseer of the Lord's work; who is to be called MASTER by those that work under him. The Craftsmen are to avoid all ill language, and to call each other by no disobliging name, but Brother or Fellow, and to behave themselves courteously within and without the lodge.

The Master knowing himself to be able of cunning, shall undertake the Lord's work as reasonably as possible, and truly dispend his goods as if they were his own; nor to give more wages to any Brother or Apprentice than he really may deserve.

Both the Master and the Masons receiving their wages justly, shall be faithful to the Lord, and honestly finish their work, whether task or journey; nor put the work to task that hath been accustomed to journey.

None shall discover envy at the prosperity of a Brother, nor supplant him, or put him out of his work, if he be capable to finish the same; for no man can finish another's work so much to the Lord's profit, unless he be thoroughly acquainted with the designs and drafts of him that began it.

When a Fellow-Craftsman is chosen Warden of the work under the Master, he shall be true both to Master and Fellows, shall carefully oversee the work in the Master's absence to the Lord's profit; and his Brethren shall obey him.

All Masons employed shall meekly receive their wages, without murmuring or mutiny, and not desert the Master till the work is finished.

2

A younger Brother shall be instructed in working, to prevent spoiling the materials for want of judgment, and for increasing and continuing of Brotherly Love.

All the tools used in working shall be approved by the Grand Lodge.

No laborer shall be employed in the proper work of Masonry; nor shall *Free Masons* work with those that are not free, without an urgent necessity; nor shall they teach laborers and unaccepted Masons as they should teach a Brother or Fellow.

VI.—OF BEHAVIOR.

1.—*In the Lodge while constituted.*

You are not to hold private committees or separate conversation, without leave from the Master, nor to talk of any thing impertinent or unseemly, nor interrupt the Master or Wardens, or any Brother speaking to the Master: Nor behave yourself ludicrously or jestingly while the Lodge is engaged in what is serious and solemn; nor use any unbecoming language upon any pretence whatsoever; but to pay due reverence to your Master, Wardens and Fellows, and put them to worship.

If any complaint be brought, the Brother found guilty shall stand to the award and determination of the Lodge, who are the proper and competent judges of all such controversies, (unless you carry it by appeal to the Grand Lodge,) and to whom they ought to be referred, unless a Lord's work be hindered the mean while, in which case a particular reference may be made; but you must never go to law about what concerneth MASONRY, without an absolute necessity, apparent to the Lodge.

2.--*Behavior after the Lodge is over, and the Brethren not gone.*

You may enjoy yourselves with innocent mirth, treating one another according to ability, but avoiding all excess, or forcing any Brother to eat or drink beyond his inclination, or hindering him from going when his occasions call him, or doing or saying any thing offensive, or that may forbid an EASY and FREE conversation; for that would blast our harmony, and defeat our laudable purposes. Therefore no private piques or quarrels must be brought within the door of the Lodge, far less any quarrels about religion, or nations, or State policy, we being only, as Masons, of the Catholic religion above mentioned; we are also of all nations, tongues, kindreds and languages, and are resolved against *all politics*, as what never yet conduced to the welfare of the Lodge, nor ever will. This *Charge* has been always strictly enjoined and observed; but especially ever since the Reformation in Britain, or the dissent and secession of these nations from the communion of Rome.

3.--*Behavior when Brethren meet without Strangers, but not in a Lodge formed.*

You are to salute one another in a courteous manner, as you will be instructed, calling each other BROTHER, freely giving mutual instruction as shall be thought expedient, without being overseen or overheard, and without encroaching upon each other, or derogating from that respect which is due to any Brother, were he not a Mason: for though all Masons are as Brethren upon the same Level, yet Masonry takes no honor from a man that he had before; nay, rather it adds to his honor, especially if he has deserved well of the

Brotherhood, who **must** give honor to whom **it** is due, and avoid ill manners.

4.—*Behavior* **in** *Presence* **of** *Strangers not Masons.*

You **shall be** cautious in your words and carriage, that the most penetrating stranger shall not be able to discover or **find out what is not proper to** be intimated; and sometimes **you shall divert** a discourse, and manage **it** prudently for the **honor of** the Worshipful Fraternity.

5.—*Behavior at Home and in your Neighborhood.*

You **are to act as becomes a moral and wise man,** particularly not **to let your family, friends and** neighbors know the concerns of the Lodge, etc., **but wisely** to consult **your** own honor, and that of the Ancient Brotherhood, **for** reasons not to be mentioned here. You must also consult your health, by not continuing together too late, or too long from home, after lodge hours are past; and by avoiding of gluttony or drunkenness, that your families be not neglected or injured, **nor you disabled from working.**

6.—*Behavior towards a Strange Brother.*

You **are cautiously to examine** him, in such a method as **prudence shall direct** you, that you may not be imposed upon **by an ignorant false pretender, whom** you are to reject with **contempt and derision, and** beware of giving him any hints of knowledge.

But if you discover him to be **a** true and genuine Brother, you are to respect him accordingly; and if he is in want, you must relieve him, if you can, or else direct him how he may **be relieved:** You must employ him some days, or else recom-

mend him to be employed.   But you are not charged to do
beyond your ability, only to prefer a poor Brother, that is a
good man and true, before any other poor people in the same
circumstances

Finally, All these CHARGES you are to observe, and also
those that shall be communicated to you in another way;
cultivating Brotherly Love, the foundation and cape-stone,
the cement and glory of this ancient Fraternity; avoiding all
wrangling and quarreling, all slander and backbiting, nor
permitting others to slander any honest Brother, but defend-
ing his character, and doing him all good offices, as far as is
consistent with your honor and safety, and no farther.   And
if any of them do you injury, you must apply to your own or
his Lodge, and from thence you may appeal to the Grand
Lodge at the quarterly communication, and from thence to
the Annual Grand Lodge, as has been the ancient laudable
conduct of our forefathers in every nation; never taking a
legal course, but when the case cannot be otherwise decided,
and patiently listening to the honest and friendly advice of
Master and Fellows, when they would prevent your going to
law with strangers, or would excite you to put a speedy
period to all lawsuits, that so you may mind the affair of
Masonry with the more alacrity and success; but with respect
to Brothers or Fellows at law, the Master and Brethren
should kindly offer their mediation, which ought to be thank-
fully submitted to by the contending Brethren; and if that
submission is impracticable, they must, however, carry on
their process, or lawsuit, without wrath and rancor, (not in

the common way,) saying or doing nothing which may hinder Brotherly Love, and **good** offices to be renewed and continued; that all may see the benign influence of **Masonry**, as all true Masons have done from the beginning of the world, and will do to the end of time. AMEN. *So mote it be.*

------◆------

GENERAL REGULATIONS,

COMPILED first by Mr. GEORGE PAYNE, *Anno* 1720, when he was Grand Master, and approved by the Grand Lodge on St. JOHN Baptist's Day, *Anno* 1721, at Stationer's Hall, London; when the most noble Prince JOHN, *Duke of Montagu,* was unanimously chosen our Grand Master for the year ensuing; who chose JOHN BEAL, M. D., his Deputy Grand Master; and Mr. JOSIAH VILLE-NEAU and Mr. THOMAS MORRIS, Jun., were chosen by the Lodge Grand Wardens. And now, by the command of our said Right Worshipful Grand Master MONTAGU, the *Author* of this book has compared them with, and reduced them to the ancient *Records* and immemorial *Usages* of the Fraternity, and digested them into this new method, with several proper Explications, for the use of the Lodges in and about London and Westminster.

I. THE Grand Master or his Deputy hath authority and right not only to be present in any true Lodge, but also to preside wherever he is, with the Master of the Lodge on his left hand, and to order his Grand Wardens to attend him, who are not to act in particular Lodges as Wardens, but in his presence, and at his command; because there the Grand Master may command the Wardens of that Lodge, or any other Brethren he pleaseth, to attend and act as his Wardens *pro tempore*.

II. The Master of a particular Lodge has the right and authority of congregating the members of his Lodge into a Chapter at pleasure, upon any emergency or occurrence, as well as to appoint the time and place of their usual forming; and in case of sickness, death, or necessary absence of the Master, the Senior Warden shall act as Master *pro tempore*, if no Brother is present who has been Master of that Lodge before; for in that case the absent Master's authority reverts to the last Master then present; though he cannot act until the said Senior Warden has once congregated the Lodge, or, in his absence, the Junior Warden.

III. The Master of each particular Lodge, or one of the Wardens, or some other Brother by his order, shall keep a book containing their By-laws, the names of their members, with a list of all the Lodges in town, and the usual times and places of their forming, and all their transactions that are proper to be written.

IV. No Lodge shall make more than FIVE new Brethren at one time, nor any man under the age of twenty-five, who must be also his own master, unless by a Dispensation from the Grand Master or his Deputy.

V. No man can be made or admitted a member of a particular Lodge, without previous notice one month before given to the said Lodge, in order to make due inquiry into the reputation and capacity of the candidate; unless by the Dispensation aforesaid.

VI. But no man can be entered a Brother in any particular Lodge, or admitted to be a member thereof, without the unanimous consent **of all** the **members of that Lodge** then present when the candidate is proposed, and their **consent is** formally asked **by** the Master; **and they are to** signify their consent or **dissent** in their own prudent **way, either** virtually **or in form, but** with unanimity: **Nor is** this inherent privilege subject to a Dispensation; **because the** members of **a particular Lodge are the** best judges **of it; and** if a fractious **member should be imposed on** them, it might **spoil** their harmony or hinder their freedom; **or even break or** disperse **the Lodge, which ought to be avoided by all good** and true **Brethren.**

VII. **Every new Brother at his** making is decently to clothe the Lodge—that is, all the Brethren present—and to deposit something for the relief of indigent and decayed Brethren, as **the** candidate shall think fit to bestow, over **and** above the **small allowance** stated by **the** By-laws of that particular **Lodge; which charity** shall **be** lodged with **the** Master or **Wardens, or the cashier, if** the members think fit to choose one. **And the candidate shall** also solemnly promise **to** submit **to** the **Constitutions, the Charges and** Regulations, and to such other good **Usages as shall be intimated to them in time and** place convenient.

VIII. **No set or number of Brethren shall withdraw or separate themselves from the Lodge in which they were** made Brethren, **or were afterwards admitted members, unless** the Lodge becomes **too** numerous; **nor even then without a** Dispensation from the Grand **Master or** his **Deputy; and** when they are thus separated, they **must either** immediately join themselves to such other Lodge as they shall like best, with the unanimous consent of that other Lodge to which they go, (as above regulated,) or else they must obtain the Grand Master's Warrant to join in forming a new lodge.

If any set or number of Masons shall take upon themselves to form a Lodge without the Grand Master's Warrant, the regular lodges are not to countenance them, nor own them as fair Brethren and duly formed, nor approve of their acts and deeds; but must treat them as rebels, until they humble themselves, as the Grand Master shall in his prudence direct, and until he approve of them by his Warrant, which must be signified to the other lodges, as the custom is when a new lodge is to be registered in the *List of Lodges.*

IX. But if any Brother so far misbehave himself as to render his Lodge uneasy, he shall be twice duly admonished by the Master or Wardens in a formed lodge; and if he will not refrain his imprudence, and obediently submit to the advice of the Brethren, and reform what gives them offence, he shall be dealt with according to the By-laws of that particular Lodge, or else in such a manner as the Quarterly Communication shall in their great prudence think fit; for which a new Regulation may be afterwards made.

X. The majority of every particular lodge, when congregated, shall have the privilege of giving instructions to their Master and Wardens, before the assembling of the Grand Chapter or Lodge, at the three Quarterly Communications hereafter mentioned, and of the Annual Grand Lodge too; because their Masters and Wardens are their representatives, and are supposed to speak their mind.

XI. All particular lodges are to observe the same Usages as much as possible; in order to which, and for cultivating a good understanding among Freemasons, some members **out** of every lodge shall be deputed to visit the other lodges as often as shall be thought convenient.

XII. The GRAND LODGE consists of, and is formed by the Masters and Wardens of **all** the regular particular lodges upon record, with the Grand Master at their head, and his Deputy on his left hand, and the Grand Wardens in their proper places, and must have a Quarterly Communication about Michaelmas, Christmas, and Lady-day, in some convenient place, as the Grand Master shall appoint, where no Brother shall be present who **is** not at that time a member thereof, without a Dispensation; and while he stays, **he shall** not be allowed to vote, nor even give his opinion, without leave of the Grand Lodge, asked and given, or unless it be duly asked by the said lodge.

All matters are to be determined in the Grand Lodge by a majority of votes, each member having one vote, and the Grand Master having two votes, unless the said lodge leave any particular thing to the determination of the Grand Master for the sake of expedition.

XIII. At the said Quarterly Communication, all matters that concern the Fraternity in general, or particular Lodges, or single Brethren, are quietly, sedately, and maturely to be discoursed of and transacted: Apprentices must be admitted Masters and Fellow Craft only here, unless by a Dispensation. Here also all differences that cannot be made up and accommodated privately, nor by a particular Lodge, are to be seriously considered and decided: And if any Brother thinks himself aggrieved by the decision of this Board, he may appeal to the Annual Grand Lodge next ensuing, and leave his appeal in writing with the Grand Master, or his Deputy, or the Grand Wardens.

Here, also, the Master or the Wardens of each particular Lodge shall bring and produce a list of such members as have been made, or even admitted, in their particular lodges since the last communication of the Grand Lodge: and there shall be a book kept by the Grand Master or his Deputy, or rather by some brother whom the Grand Lodge shall appoint for Secretary, wherein shall be recorded *all the Lodges*, with their usual times and places of forming, and the names of all the members of each Lodge; and all the affairs of the Grand Lodge that are proper to be written.

They shall also consider of the most prudent and effectual methods of collecting and disposing of what money shall be given to or lodged with them in Charity, towards the relief only of any true Brother fallen into poverty or decay, but of none else: But every particular Lodge shall dispose of their own Charity for poor Brethren, according to their own By-laws, until it be agreed by all the lodges (in a new Regulation) to carry in the Charity collected by them to the Grand Lodge, at the Quarterly or Annual Communication, in order to make a common stock of it, for the more handsome relief of poor Brethren.

They shall also appoint a Treasurer, a Brother of good worldly substance, who shall be a member of the Grand Lodge by virtue of his office, and shall be always present,

and have power to move to the Grand **Lodge** anything, especially what concerns his office.   To him shall be committed all
money raised for Charity, or for any other use of the Grand
Lodge, which **he** shall write down in a book, with the respective ends and uses for which the several sums are intended; and
shall expend and disburse the same by such a certain order
signed, as the Grand Lodge shall afterwards agree to in a
new Regulation: **But he** shall not vote in choosing a Grand
Master or Wardens, though in every other transaction.   **As**
in like manner the Secretary shall be a member of the Grand
Lodge by virtue of his office, **and** vote in everything, except
in choosing a Grand Master or **Wardens.**

The Treasurer and Secretary shall have each **a clerk, who**
must be a Brother and Fellow Craft, but never must be **a**
member of the Grand Lodge, nor speak without being allowed
or desired.

The Grand Master, or his Deputy, shall always command
the Treasurer and Secretary, with their clerks and books, in
order to see how matters go on, and to know what is expe-
dient to be done upon any emergent occasion.

Another Brother (who must be a Fellow Craft) should be
appointed to look after the door of the Grand Lodge, but
shall be no member of it.

But these offices may be farther explained by a new Regulation, when the necessity and expediency of **them may**
more appear than at present **to the** Fraternity.

XIV. If at any Grand Lodge, stated or occasional, quarterly or annual, the Grand Master and **his** Deputy should be
both absent, then the present **Master** of **a** Lodge, that has

been the longest a Freemason, shall take the chair, and preside as Grand Master *pro tempore*, and shall be vested with all his power and honor for the time: provided there is no Brother present that has been Grand Master formerly, or Deputy Grand Master; for the last Grand Master present, or else the last Deputy present, should always of right take place in the absence of the present Grand Master and his Deputy.

XV. In the Grand Lodge none can act as Wardens but the Grand Wardens themselves, if present; and, if absent, the Grand Master, or the person who presides in his place, shall order private Wardens to act as Grand Wardens *pro tempore*, whose places are to be supplied by two Fellow Craft of the same Lodge, called forth to act, or sent thither by the particular Master thereof; or if by him omitted, then they shall be called by the Grand Master, that so the Grand Lodge may be always complete.

XVI. The Grand Wardens, or any others, are first to advise with the Deputy about the affairs of the Lodge or of the Brethren, and not to apply to the Grand Master without the knowledge of the Deputy, unless he refuse his concurrence in any certain necessary affair; in which case, or in case of any difference between the Deputy and the Grand Wardens, or other Brethren, both parties are to go by concert to the Grand Master, who can easily decide the controversy and make up the difference by virtue of his great authority.

The Grand Master should receive no intimation of business concerning Masonry but from his Deputy first, except in such certain cases as his Worship can well judge of; for if the application to the Grand Master be irregular, he can easily order the Grand Wardens, or any other Brethren thus applying, to wait upon his Deputy, who is to prepare the business speedily, and to lay it orderly before his Worship.

XVII. No Grand Master, Deputy Grand Master, Grand Wardens, Treasurer, Secretary, or whoever acts for them, or in their stead *pro tempore*, can at the same time be the Master or Warden of a particular Lodge; but as soon as any of them has honorably discharged his Grand Office, he returns to that post or station in his particular Lodge, from which he was called to officiate above.

XVIII. If the Deputy Grand Master be sick, or necessarily absent, the Grand Master may choose any Fellow Craft he please to be his Deputy *pro tempore:* But he that is chosen Deputy at the Grand Lodge, and the Grand Wardens too, cannot be discharged without the cause fairly appear to the majority of the Grand Lodge; and the Grand Master, if he is uneasy, may call a Grand Lodge on purpose to lay the cause before them, and to have their advice and concurrence: in which case, the majority of the Grand Lodge, if they cannot reconcile the Master and his Deputy or his Wardens, are to concur in allowing the Master to discharge his said Deputy or his said Wardens, and to choose another Deputy immediately; and the said Grand Lodge shall choose other Wardens in that case, that harmony and peace may be preserved.

XIX. If the Grand Master should abuse his power, and render himself unworthy of the obedience and subjection of the Lodges, he shall be treated in a way and manner to be agreed upon in a new Regulation; because hitherto the Ancient Fraternity have had no occasion for it, their former Grand Masters having all behaved themselves worthy of that honorable office.

XX. The Grand Master, with his Deputy and Wardens, shall (at least once) go round and visit all the Lodges about town during his mastership.

XXI. If the Grand Master die during his mastership, or by sickness, or by being beyond sea, or any other way should be rendered incapable of discharging his office, the Deputy, or, in his absence, the Senior Grand Warden, or, in his absence, the Junior, or, in his absence, any three present Masters of Lodges, shall join to congregate the Grand Lodge immediately, to advise together upon that emergency, and to send two of their number to invite the LAST Grand Master to resume his office, which now in course reverts to him; or, if he refuse, then the NEXT LAST, and so backward. But if no former Grand Master can be found, then the *Deputy* shall act as *Principal* until another is chosen; or, if there be no Deputy, then the oldest Master.

XXII. The BRETHREN of all the Lodges in and about London and Westminster shall meet at an *Annual Communication* and *Feast*, in some convenient place, on *St. John Baptist's* Day, or else on *St. John Evangelist's* Day, as the Grand Lodge shall think fit by a *new Regulation*, having of late years met on St. John Baptist's Day: Provided,

The *majority* of the Masters and Wardens, with the Grand Master, his Deputy and Wardens, agree at their Quarterly Communications, three months before, that there shall be a Feast and a General Communication of all the Brethren: For if either the Grand Master, or the majority of the particular Masters, are against it, it must be dropped for that time.

But whether there shall be a Feast for all the Brethren or not, yet the GRAND LODGE must meet in some convenient place *annually* on St. John's Day ; or, if it be Sunday, then on the next day, in order to choose every year a *new* Grand Master, Deputy and Wardens.

XXIII. If it be thought expedient, and the Grand Master, with the majority of the Masters and Wardens, agree to hold a Grand Feast, according to the ancient laudable custom of Masons, then the GRAND WARDENS shall have the care of preparing the tickets, sealed with the Grand Master's seal, of disposing of the tickets, of receiving the money for the tickets, of buying the materials of the Feast, of finding out a proper and convenient place to feast in, and of every other thing that concerns the entertainment.

But, that the work may not be too burdensome to the two Grand Wardens, and that all matters may be expeditiously and safely managed, the Grand Master or his Deputy shall have power to nominate and appoint a certain number of Stewards, as his Worship shall think fit, to act in concert with the two Grand Wardens; all things relating to the Feast being decided amongst them by a majority of voices, except the Grand Master or his Deputy interpose by a particular direction or appointment.

XXIV. The Wardens and STEWARDS shall in due time wait upon the Grand Master or his Deputy for directions and orders about the premises ; but if his Worship and his Deputy are sick, or necessarily absent, they shall call together the Masters and Wardens of Lodges to meet on purpose for their advice and orders; or else they may take the matter wholly upon themselves, and do the best they can.

The Grand Wardens and the Stewards are to account for all the money they receive, or expend, to the Grand Lodge, after dinner, or when the Grand Lodge shall think fit to receive their accounts.

If the Grand Master pleases, he may in due time summon all the Masters and Wardens of Lodges, to consult with them about ordering the Grand Feast, and about any emergency or accidental thing relating thereunto, that may require advice, or else to take it upon himself altogether.

XXV. The Masters of Lodges shall each appoint one experienced and discreet Fellow Craft of his Lodge, to compose a committee, consisting of one from every Lodge, who shall meet to receive, in a convenient apartment, every person that brings a ticket, and shall have power to discourse him, if they think fit, in order to admit him or debar him, as they shall see cause: *Provided* they send no man away before they have acquainted all the Brethren within doors with the reasons thereof, to avoid mistakes; that so no true Brother may be debarred, nor a false brother or mere pretender admitted. This committee must meet very early on St. John's Day at the place, even before any persons come with tickets.

XXVI. The Grand Master shall appoint two or more TRUSTY BRETHREN to be porters or door-keepers, who are also to be early at the place, for some good reasons, and who are to be at the command of the committee.

XXVII. The Grand Wardens or the Stewards shall appoint beforehand such a number of brethren to serve at table as they think fit and proper for that work; and they may advise with the Masters and Wardens of Lodges about the most proper persons, if they please, or may take in such by their recommendation; for none are to serve that day but Free and Accepted Masons, that the communication may be free and harmonious.

XXVIII. All the members of the Grand Lodge must be at the place long before dinner, with the Grand Master or his Deputy at their head, who shall retire, and form themselves. And this is done in order—

1. To receive any appeals, duly lodged, as above regulated, that the appellant may be heard, and the affair may be amicably decided before dinner, if possible; but if it cannot, it must be delayed till after the new Grand Master is elected; and if it cannot be decided after dinner, it may be delayed, and referred to a particular committee, that shall quietly adjust it, and make report to the next Quarterly Communication, that Brotherly Love may be preserved.

2. To prevent any difference or disgust which may be feared to arise that day, that no interruption may be given to the harmony and pleasure of the Grand Feast.

3. To consult about whatever concerns the decency and decorum of the Grand Assembly, and to prevent all indecency and ill manners, the assembly being promiscuous.

4. To receive and consider of any good motion, or any momentous and important affair, that shall be brought from the particular lodges by their representatives, their several Masters and Wardens.

XXIX. After these things are discussed, the Grand Master and his Deputy, the Grand Wardens or the Stewards, the Secretary, the Treasurer, the clerks, and every other person shall withdraw, and leave the Masters and Wardens of the particular lodges alone, in order to consult amicably about electing a new Grand Master, or continuing the present, if they have not done it the day before; and if they are unanimous for continuing the present Grand Master, his Worship shall be called in, and humbly desired to do the Fraternity the honor of ruling them for the year ensuing: And after dinner it will be known whether he accepts of it or not: for it should not be discovered but by the election itself.

XXX. Then the Masters and Wardens, and all the Brethren, may converse promiscuously, or as they please to sort together, until the dinner is coming in, when every Brother takes his seat at table.

XXXI. Some time after dinner, the Grand Lodge is formed, not in the retirement, but in the presence of all the Brethren, who yet are not members of it, and must not therefore speak until they are desired and allowed.

XXXII. If the Grand Master of last year has consented with the Master and Wardens in private, before dinner, to continue for the year ensuing, then one of the Grand Lodge, deputed for that purpose, shall represent to all the Brethren his Worship's good government, etc. And, turning to him, shall, in the name of the Grand Lodge, humbly request him to do the Fraternity the great honor, (if nobly born, if not,) the great kindness of continuing to be their Grand Master for the year ensuing. And his Worship declaring his consent by

a bow or a speech, as he pleases, the said deputed member
of the Grand Lodge shall proclaim him Grand Master, and
all the members of the Lodge shall salute him in due form.
And all the Brethren shall for a few minutes have leave to
declare their satisfaction, pleasure, and congratulation.

XXXIII. But if either the Master and Wardens have not
in private, this day before dinner, nor the day before, desired
the *last* Grand Master to continue in the mastership another
year; or if he, when desired, has not consented; then

The *last* Grand Master shall nominate his successor for
the year ensuing, who, if unanimously approved by the
Grand Lodge, and, if there present, shall be proclaimed,
saluted, and congratulated the new Grand Master, as above
hinted, and immediately installed by the last Grand Master,
according to Usage.

XXXIV. But if that nomination is not unanimously approved, the new Grand Master shall be chosen immediately
by ballot, every Master and Warden writing his man's name,
and the last Grand Master writing his man's name too; and
the man whose name the last Grand Master shall first take
out, casually or by chance, shall be Grand Master for the
year ensuing; and, if present, he shall be proclaimed, saluted,
and congratulated, as above hinted, and forthwith installed
by the last Grand Master, according to Usage.

XXXV. The last Grand Master thus continued, or the
NEW Grand Master thus installed, shall next nominate and
appoint his Deputy Grand Master, either the last or a new
one, who shall be also declared, saluted, and congratulated,
as above hinted.

The Grand Master shall also nominate the new Grand Wardens, and, if unanimously approved by the Grand Lodge, shall be declared, saluted, and congratulated, as above hinted; but if not, they shall be chosen by ballot, in the same way as the Grand Master: As the Wardens of private lodges are also to be chosen by ballot in each Lodge, if the members thereof do not agree to their Master's nomination.

XXXVI. But if the Brother whom the present Grand Master shall nominate for his successor, or whom the majority of the Grand Lodge shall happen to choose by ballot, is, by sickness or other necessary occasion, absent from the Grand Feast, he cannot be proclaimed the new Grand Master, unless the old Grand Master, or some of the Masters and Wardens of the Grand Lodge can vouch, upon the honor of a brother, that the said person, so nominated or chosen, will readily accept of the said office; in which case the old Grand Master shall act as proxy, and shall nominate the Deputy and Wardens in his name, and in his name also receive the usual honors, homage, and congratulation.

XXXVII. Then the Grand Master shall allow any Brother, Fellow Craft, or Apprentice to speak, directing his discourse to his Worship; or to make any motion for the good of the Fraternity, which shall be either immediately considered and finished, or else referred to the consideration of the Grand Lodge at their next communication, stated or occasional. When that is over,

XXXVIII. The Grand Master or his Deputy, or some Brother appointed by him, shall harangue all the Brethren, and give them good advice: And, lastly, after some other transactions, that cannot be written in any language, the Brethren may go away or stay longer, as they please.

XXXIX. Every Annual Grand Lodge has an inherent power and authority to make new Regulations, or to alter these, for the real benefit of this ancient Fraternity: Provided always that the old Landmarks be carefully preserved, and that such alterations and new Regulations be proposed and agreed to at the third quarterly communication preceding the Annual Grand Feast; and that they be offered also to the perusal of all the Brethren before dinner, in writing, even of the youngest Apprentice; the approbation and consent of the majority of all the Brethren present being absolutely necessary to make the same binding and obligatory; which must, after dinner, and after the new Grand Master is installed, be solemnly desired; as it was desired and obtained for these Regulations, when proposed by the Grand Lodge, to about 150 Brethren, on St. John Baptist's Day, 1721.

With the authorities here given, the Constitutions of his Grand Lodge, and the By-laws of the Lodge which he governs, the Master ought to be able to solve most, if not all, of the questions that present themselves in the ordinary course of events.

In the succeeding chapters we shall endeavor to demonstrate their application to the prominent topics of the institution.

CHAPTER II.

Laws relating to Candidates.

SECTION I.—QUALIFICATIONS.

MASONRY, like society in general, is an aggregate of individuals, and exercises, as a body, the sovereignty primarily invested in the individual Masons. The source of power being in the people, it is important to consider who are the proper persons to be admitted among us, and the qualifications which are indispensable to the success of an application for admission.

The applicant must be *free-born,* "having no maim or defect in his body, that may render him uncapable of learning the art, and being made a brother."

He must be of *lawful age;* that is, at least twenty-one years; nor can any authority change or remove this requirement. It is the custom in Europe to admit the son of a Mason, who is called a *lewis* or *louveteau,* and members of the royal family, at the age of eighteen; but in this country we regard Masonry as of too serious a character to be intrusted to boys, and hence we follow the rule in its integrity.

He must be *under the tongue of good report;* that is to say, of good moral character and standing in the community, and **have a** visible and **honorable** means of obtaining a livelihood for himself and those **who** may be dependent upon him.

He must acknowledge and declare *his belief in* **the** *existence* **of a** *Supreme* **Being, and a future state** *of* *existence;* **and that not only does** he seek admission **of his own free will and accord,** but that he is not in- **cited thereto by the solicitation of** friends, nor by the inducement of mercenary or **other** unworthy motives.

He must **be a** resident **of the place in** which **he** seeks **to be initiated. In other countries than** our own, this law is **not** acknowledged, and, **indeed, it is to be admitted** that until **about the** year 1848 **it was unknown here. The** regulation **is** now, **however, in** force throughout the United States—exceptions being generally made **in** the case of mariners in **the actual practice of** their profession, and officers in the mili- **tary or naval service of the general** government—and **has arisen from the necessities of our** contiguous jurisdictions; **the increase of lodges often** bringing those **of neighboring** States in close **proximity** to the line on **either side, which,** together with the facilities **of travel, have often given rise to unpleasant feelings between the brethren, by the working up in one juris- diction of** material belonging to **another. The great evil of the** indiscriminate **making of** Masons without **regard to** their place of residence, **has been the** facility thus afforded to men who had no characters to lose at home, going abroad, and palming themselves off on some new-found acquaintance as suitable candidates for the honors of Masonry; obtaining, by indirection, what would have been promptly refused them where they were known, and thus committing a fraud upon the Craft. For this, and for other reasons that will appear in their proper place, the law has become general that a man can only be initiated in the lodge nearest his place of residence, within the Masonic jurisdiction in which he has his legal home.

He should have a fixed and steady purpose in his own mind that, in uniting himself with the Masonic fraternity, thus becoming part of an association dating in principle from the earliest civilization, and always found engaged in the endeavor to enfranchise the spirit of man from the bonds of ignorance and error, he does so with a desire to extend the sphere of his own usefulness, and to derive happiness from the effort to increase the happiness of others. He should consider that in a society existing wherever civilization extends, and embracing within its membership men of every station in life, there must necessarily be some with whom he would not willingly associate; and yet, once received, they will be his brethren, and have the right to claim his assistance and protection, should they be in distress from legitimate causes,

3

and thus he must be prepared to exercise the virtue of self-abnegation.

He should also understand that, as a Mason, it will be his duty to examine into and study the history and ethics of the society, that he may be prepared to discharge the functions and duties that may be laid upon him, from which it follows that he should have received at least a moderate degree of mental culture; be capable of reading, that he may enrich his own mind; of writing, that he may communicate his thoughts to others, and thus help to increase the general store of knowledge, not hiding his light under a bushel, nor remaining satisfied to be a hewer of wood and drawer of water, but striving to improve the talent committed to him, for his own advancement and that of the fraternity.

The candidate, thus qualified, proceeds in the steps necessary to his acceptance and subsequent progress, by subscribing to, and causing to be presented to the nearest Lodge, his petition, which we now proceed to consider.

SECTION II.—THE PETITION.

It was the custom in olden times—and the rule is still in force, though sadly neglected—that a person desirous of being made a Mason should present *a petition* to the Lodge in which he desired to be initiated. In many lodges, the practice now is, for a

member to rise in his place, and say, "I propose Mr.
...... for initiation in this Lodge;" or the name of
the candidate, with his age, occupation, etc., is handed
to the Secretary, in which case the formula is varied
by his saying, "Brother Blank proposes Mr. ......,"
etc. This is not only a loose way of doing business,
but is positively unmasonic; because it has always
been required that the candidate should present a
petition, signed with his full name, and recommended
by two brethren, as an evidence that the act was one
of his own free-will, and with a distinct understanding of what he proposed to do. The document itself
should be preserved in the archives of the Lodge, as
an evidence of the jurisdiction acquired by the Lodge
in the premises. It may be in the following or some
similar form :

" *To the Worshipful Master, Wardens and Brethren of* .....
Lodge, No. ....., *of Free and Accepted Masons.*

"THE undersigned petitioner respectfully sheweth, that
having long entertained a favorable opinion of your ancient
institution, he now voluntarily offers himself as a candidate
for initiation and membership in your Lodge. He is .....
years of age; his occupation ......; resides ......

(Signed) "A. B."

RECOMMENDED BY
Bro. ....
Bro. ....

This petition* must be read at a stated meeting of the Lodge : no business relating to the petition of or ballot for a candidate can be transacted at a special meeting. The reason for this is found in the Fifth and Sixth of the Thirty-nine Articles cited in the preceding chapter, namely, that all the brethren may have timely notice, and, by inquiry into the character and habits of the petitioner, be prepared to prevent a fractious or unwholesome member being imposed upon the Lodge. If it is decided to receive the petition, it is then entered upon the record, and referred to a committee for investigation. It has now become the property of the Lodge, and cannot be withdrawn, but must take the usual course by report of committee and ballot. It is the duty of the committee not only to satisfy themselves that the candidate is in possession of the necessary qualifications, but that he has not previously been rejected by any other Lodge ; for in that case, he could not be received (without the consent of the rejecting Lodge, and not even then,) till after the lapse of a certain time provided for in

---

* In the majority of lodges it is required that the petition should be accompanied by a fee—usually five dollars—as an earnest of the sincerity of the petitioner. It has been decided, however, that the money so deposited does not become the property of the lodge till action has been taken on the petition, the understanding being that, in case of rejection, the fee shall be returned.—*G. L. of N. Y.*, 1859.

the local regulations of the several Grand Lodges—
six months in some, one year in others. The reason
for this may be found in the Fifth of the Ancient
Charges :—" None shall discover envy at the prosperity of a brother, nor supplant him, or put him out
of his work, if he be capable to finish the same ; for
no man can finish another's work so much to the
Lord's profit, unless he be thoroughly acquainted with
the designs and draughts of him that began it."
Practically, however, it arises from the necessities of
multiplied lodges and jurisdictions. Its intention is,
not only to preserve harmony among the lodges, but
to shield the Craft against the wiles of improper persons, determined to force themselves upon it at all
hazards. In ninety-nine cases out of a hundred, the
rejected candidate and his friends feel that a grievous
injustice has been done him, and, in the spirit of
human nature, set about the discovery of some means
of retaliation. Without stopping to point out the
unjustifiable and unmasonic nature of such proceedings, it is only necessary to say, that although, in
some cases, there may be injustice—for Masons are
not devoid of failings—it must not be forgotten that
the ballot, being " strictly and inviolably secret," we
cannot lawfully inquire into the cause of rejection,
and can, therefore, only deal with it as a fact for
which we are not responsible. Moreover, it is always

of greater importance that the Craft should be protected against the admission of improper material,
and that peace and harmony should be preserved in
the Lodge, than it is that any man, however distinguished, should be admitted to its privileges; hence
the legal delay can never work harm, nor can there
be any shadow of injustice in allowing the Lodge to
which the application was first made, and that thus
acquired jurisdiction, to retain it, till time and investigation shall have convinced them of the propriety
of their first act, or of its reversal, on the presentation of a new petition. Mistakes are common to all
men and bodies of men, and it does sometimes happen that a black ball is cast in error, as in a case of
mistaken identity; but this does not alter the fact
of the rejection, nor is there any remedy but the
presentation of a new petition when the proper time
has arrived. In this connection it is proper to remark, that the candidate, when waited upon by the
committee, must—as the lawyers say—well and truly
answer all questions that may be put to him touching
the matter in hand; for it is a well-settled principle
that a Mason may be disciplined for an offence committed previous to his initiation, a knowledge of which
was willfully concealed at the time of his making.—
(*G. L. of N. Y.*, 1861.) Thus, a person who had
applied to a lodge, and been rejected, and who, on

his application to another lodge, concealed that fact, might, and ought to be disciplined for the deception so practiced; for although, as a profane, he was not amenable to Masonic law, he was bound to act as an honest man, in whose lexicon false pretences have no place.

SECTION III.—THE BALLOT.

Assuming the committee to have made its report, favorable or otherwise, the next step is the ballot, which is now the universal method by which the brethren express their acceptance or rejection of a candidate; for the ancient regulations do not specify any particular mode of voting, but only that it shall be done prudently and with unanimity. The first and most important consideration in connection with the ballot is, that it shall not be taken till one month after the reception of the petition. We are aware that the practice is to ballot, in most lodges, at the expiration of two weeks, and in some cases *one week*, which is in accordance with the local regulations of many Grand Lodges, the letter of such regulations being, that "a petition for initiation or affiliation can only be received at a stated communication, and must be laid over till the following one; which correctly answered the requirements when lodges met but once a month; but now, when nine lodges out of ten meet twice in each month, and many four times.

the letter may still be adhered to, but the spirit is certainly violated. The ancient rule, to be found in the General Regulations of 1721, that "no man can be made or admitted a member of a particular lodge without previous notice, one month before given to the said lodge," is still in force; and, if not absolutely a landmark, is at all events a law of universal acceptance and observance, except in the United States. The Constitution of New York (to which we refer because we are best acquainted with it) cites, as a landmark, that "a candidate must be proposed in open lodge, at a stated meeting, and can only be accepted at a stated meeting following;" nothing being said of the lapse of "one month," found in the old regulation above quoted, from which it professes to be taken; but in 1858 the Grand Master decided that a proposition for honorary membership must lie over for one month. Now, if the empty privileges of honorary membership require a month's consideration on the part of the lodge conferring them, surely the important act of receiving a profane into active membership ought, at least, to be as maturely considered. A majority of the Grand Lodges we are, however, happy to say, enforce the rule in its integrity, and that they are right in so doing, there can be no question.

There must be a ballot: for it is the right of every

member to express his acquiescence in the admission of the petitioner, or his refusal of that admission, as his judgment may dictate; and that, too, with entire independence of any responsibility, save that due to his own conscience. If it be held that an unfavorable report is equivalent to a rejection, and that there is no need of a ballot, by a parity of reasoning it might be said that a favorable report insures an election, and thus do away with the ballot altogether.

The ballot must be unanimous.—In Europe the practice is, to require three or more negative ballots for a rejection; but as the oldest law we know of requires unanimity, and we desire to "stand on the old ways," our rule is, that without unanimity, no candidate can be accepted.

All the Brethren present must vote.—In so important a matter as the admission of a new member, it is evident that all present should participate, because it is the duty of every member to see that, so far as his influence goes, no unworthy person is admitted to membership; because, if only a portion of the members vote, the old regulation, requiring the unanimous consent of all present, cannot be complied with. It is true, that by unanimous consent a Brother may be excused from voting, but, in that case, the Lodge assumes the responsibility, and it is no longer the act of a single individual.

The ballot must be secret.—Without this indispensable quality, its purity and independence cannot be preserved; hence it is that no Brother has a right to expose the manner of his ballot, or to make known afterward how he has voted; for otherwise the harmony of the Lodge would be disturbed, and the conscientious restriction that now rests upon every Brother as he approaches the ballot-box would be removed. The exposure of the ballot may, under certain circumstances, be made a cause for discipline.

The ballot cannot be unreasonably postponed.—That is, in the ordinary course of affairs, a motion to postpone the ballot should not be entertained, because, in that case, some brother may be deprived of his right, and ultimately an unworthy or "fractious member be imposed on them." But for reasonable cause, a ballot might be postponed, though not to a distant period of time.

An unfavorable ballot cannot be reconsidered.—When after the usual course the ballot is pronounced unfavorable, the petition must also be declared rejected, and that is the end of it until the regulations of the Grand Lodge allow its presentation anew. Hence, no motion to reconsider can be entertained; but if, before the declaration of the state of the ballot, and before any of the brethren participating in it shall have left the Lodge, the Master, to avoid the possibility of mistake, or for other reasons, which to his judgment seem proper, shall see fit to cause it to be passed again, or even a third time, it is his undoubted prerogative to do so, though it is recommended that if, on the second ballot, the result still appear unfavorable, it should then cease, and the formal declaration be made.

When the ballot is held on an application for affiliation, the same rules apply, but there is no delay required in the presentation of a new application. In such case, however, the Master should cause the petition to lie over at least one regular meeting, that all the Brethren may have an opportunity to express their wishes. It will also be understood that although a petition may be presented at any time, the Lodge may always decide whether it will or will not receive it.

It is now generally admitted that a ballot for each degree is an undeniable right when demanded; but when the ballot for the first degree has been had, the Lodge may refuse another for that degree, unless cause be shown. Although, in regard to the last position, such is the decision (several times affirmed) of our mother Grand Lodge, we cannot, after mature reflection, say that we approve it. The old regulation says, that "no man can be entered a brother in any particular Lodge, or be admitted a member thereof, without the unanimous consent of all the members of that Lodge, then present when the candidate is *proposed*, and their consent is formally asked by the Master." There is, we think, a misunderstanding as to the purport of the word "proposed,"—it being generally taken in its modern sense, with reference to the first proposition, or, more properly, presentation of the petition, and not to the actual making. But we have already shown that the present fashion of proposing a candidate is of modern origin, and, like many similar innovations, has crept into our lodges with the initiation of persons previously affiliated in other associations. The proposition here referred to is, beyond doubt, that made by the Master when the candidate, having petitioned for initiation, the petition having been received, and referred to the usual committee, the committee having reported, and the ballot having proved favorable, and the candidate having presented himself for initiation, he asks the formal consent of the Lodge to proceed to that ceremony. Under these circumstances, it would clearly be the right of any brother to object to further proceeding, and the objection would have to be respected; otherwise the harmony of the Lodge would be destroyed and a brother be offended, and perhaps driven out of the Lodge, for the sake of a profane. Such is the almost universal decision of the authorities in the United States, and we agree with them.

The ballot is of such paramount importance, that, in concluding this chapter, we trust to be pardoned for detaining the reader with a few considerations connected with the use of the black ball. The negative ballot has been aptly termed the palladium of Masonry; for on its discreet use the institution relies as a safeguard against the unworthy, who seek admission to our temples for purposes utterly foreign to the designs laid down upon the original trestle-boards of the Craft. The more popular Masonry becomes, the greater will be the number of the profane, finding much in it to admire, nothing to condemn, and everything to gain by affiliation with it; and the greater will be the necessity for some one in each Lodge to stand guard over the sanctuary, armed with an instrument that shall execute his will,

"As lightning does the will of God."

Such, in the hands of a true and trusty brother, is the black-ball. Well would it be for Masonry if no others used it; well would it be for Masons if they could school their minds to a rigid respect for its appearance in the ballot, even though a brother were passing the ordeal. To these causes, more than all others, may be traced the difficulties that arise in Lodges: the scandal, the heart-burnings, the shame, that so often attend on personal quarrels, pursued to the bitter end with all the spiteful animosity arising from real or fancied injury. In the first place, then, it may be said that none but discreet brethren should assume to use this potent agent for good or evil, as the case may be: or perhaps it were better to say, that none should use it, but with the utmost discretion, as an act of conscience, in the execution of which, not even the dearest friend—no consideration of personal advantage—no fear of injury or ill-will— should for a moment be allowed to come; that, above all, it should not be used in a spirit of levity, nor from the desire to gratify a personal pique either against the petitioner or his friends; for in most cases where passion is allowed to rule, the smirk of satisfied malevolence betrays the secret. The adverse party, in the heat of disappointment, will seek a counter-revenge, and thus the fire being lighted, it will—as it has done—devastate the entire lodge, and scatter its membership, never again to be reunited. But, on the other hand, when the humblest brother knows that an applicant is unfit to be invested with the high prerogatives of the Fraternity, he should veto his admission without fear or favor. It would seem, however, that less danger is to be apprehended from the improper use of the ballot, than from the refusal of those immediately interested in the result to submit quietly to the action of the Lodge in refusing to admit to the privileges of Masonry one who, to them, may be a near and dear friend, but, to others, a manifestly improper person. Consequently, we may with propriety assert, that the duty of submission to the award of the brethren is even more important than the correct discharge of duty at the ballot-box. No man has a right to admission into the Craft, and his acceptance is, therefore, a favor granted, and not a right conceded. Why, then, should we feel aggrieved if, for good reasons, (for we are bound to believe that whoever uses the negative ballot does so with a firm conviction of the justice of his act,) the Lodge choose not to receive our friend among its members? or because all men do not place the same estimate upon him that we do? Reflection must convince us that such action cannot be justified, and that it is better to submit in silence to what we believe to be a wrong, in the hope of proving in the future the mistake of our opponents, rather than by giving way to the sudden impulses of passion, and thus, by implication, proving the unfitness of our friend by the very standard we ourselves set up. Time, that cures so many ills, will rarely fail to soothe the angry feelings and mitigate the sense of wrong, and still more rarely will it fail to do justice to the claim of any good man, whose pretensions may have been overlooked or unjustly treated. To it, when our friends have been rejected, we may safely trust, with the certainty that the delay required by our laws will never operate to the prejudice of a worthy candidate, while it may reveal a dark spot in the character of one we have deemed above reproach. Could all this be avoided, however, it would unquestionably be better; to which end we submit for consideration the method adopted by one of the French Lodges in the city of New York, which is this:—At each regular meeting of the Lodge, the Master of Ceremonies, by direction of the presiding officer, presents to each member a suitable receptacle, into which those having petitions to offer place them. These are handed to the Master, who reads them aloud, without, however, mentioning the name of the brother or brethren presenting them. The petitions then lie over for two weeks, during which time every member choosing to do so may satisfy himself as to the character and standing of the candidates, and, if desirable, see them personally. At the next meeting, opportunity is afforded to present objections, if there be any; if none are offered, then the petition goes to the committee, whose names are known only to the Master and Secretary, and takes the usual course. On the report of the committee, the Lodge proceeds to ballot, uninfluenced by any consideration but the personal character and fitness of the candidate. It is respectfully submitted that, in most, if not all cases, this plan would tend to prevent the unpleasant feelings arising from the use of the black-ball.

CHAPTER III.

The Lodge.

HAVING now disposed of the preliminary steps to the making of a Mason, some of which, in order not to break the continuity of the argument, we have followed beyond that point, we now invite attention to the formation of a Lodge, and the various considerations that pertain to its establishment.

In the third of the Ancient Charges, "a Lodge" is defined to be "a place where Masons assemble and work; hence that assembly or duly-organized society of Masons is called a *Lodge*, and every Brother ought to belong to one, and to be subject to its by-laws and the General Regulations."

Previous to the revival of Masonry in 1717, a Lodge was simply a congregation of Masons in some appropriate or convenient place, by authority of the sheriff or civil magistrate, for the purpose of "making" one or more profanes, which ceremony being accomplished, the assembly dissolved into its original elements, to meet at some future time, under like circumstances and for a similar purpose. Warrants of Constitution were then unknown, and the four old lodges that

united in the formation of the Grand Lodge of England refused to be placed under the restrictions of a
warrant—continuing their meetings by immemorial
usage and the rights they had previously acquired.
Their survivor still exists in London, and is of course
on the registry of England, but has no number, being
known as the *Lodge of Antiquity.* After the formation of the Grand Lodge of England, Warrants of
Constitution were granted directly by the Grand
Master, and such is the custom in that jurisdiction
to this day, as, indeed, in most, if not all others,
outside of the United States of America. Here the
more prudent rule obtains, of requiring new lodges
to undergo a probation, of greater or less extent, according to the local regulations of the several Grand
Lodges, as an earnest of their fitness to undertake
the labors of Masonry, and carry them forward with
profit to themselves and with honor to the Fraternity.
Let us, therefore, commence with

SECTION I.—LODGES UNDER DISPENSATION.

A Lodge under Dispensation is described as a temporary and inchoate body, not entitled to representation in the Grand Lodge, and those who work it do
not thereby forfeit their membership in any other
lodge, unless they so elect at the time when the Warrant of Constitution issues. To form such a Lodge,

it is required that a petition,* signed by not less than seven Master Masons in good and regular standing, and recommended by the nearest lodge,† be forwarded to the Grand Master, who will, if he deems it for the general interest, issue Letters of Dispensation, empowering the petitioners to meet as a regular Lodge, and perform such acts as Lodges under Dispensation may of right do, or as may be allowed by the terms of the Dispensation and the regulations of the Grand Lodge, until the next succeeding communication of the Grand Lodge, when the Dispensation ceases by its own limitation.

The powers of a Lodge under Dispensation have been the subject of much argument, and the decisions on this topic are extremely varied and conflicting. The following summary will, we think, be found to embrace the most generally received opinions:—1. A Lodge U. D. is but a committee—so to speak—of the Grand Master's selection—a temporary body, which by his prerogative he may create or dissolve at his will. 2. It can hold no regular election, nor can its officers be installed. 3. It cannot be represented in

---

* See Appendix.

† In the State of New York, no Dispensation to form a new Lodge can be issued within three months next preceding the Annual Communication of the Grand Lodge, nor without the recommendation of all the Lodges whose jurisdiction shall be affected by such Dispensation, except in cities.

Grand Lodge, because that body is composed of the Masters and Wardens of Warranted Lodges only. 4. It cannot try or discipline the Masons composing it, that being the prerogative of a Warranted Lodge. 5. It cannot form a code of By-laws. 6. It cannot affiliate Masons. 7. In the event of a warrant being refused, the property and funds must be placed in the custody of the Grand Lodge.

If these premises are correct, then Lodges U. D. are but legalized conventions for the purpose of conferring the three degrees of Masonry, and adding, to the extent of their opportunity, to the army of non-affiliated Masons. From the fifth and sixth propositions above stated, we, however, emphatically dissent. Lodges we have seen were at first fully warranted by the Grand Master; and it may safely be assumed, that when that power was surrendered to the Grand Lodge, it was in order that the whole Craft might, through their immediate representatives, have a voice in the creation of new Lodges; that when the plan of issuing Letters of Dispensation was adopted, it was that, by the acts of the new Lodge during their term of probation, the brethren assembled in Grand Lodge might be able to judge of their fitness to hold a full warrant, and become duly-constituted Lodges; that when the Grand Master issues his Dispensation for the formation of a Lodge, it is after careful exam-

ination, on his part, of all the surrounding circumstances, and with the direct expectation that, unless
through some unworthy act on the part of the Lodge,
a full warrant will be granted at the succeeding communication of the Grand Lodge. They are properly
termed *inchoate lodges*, because they are in process
of forming, or preparing for a permanent existence,
under a warrant, and they are therefore just as competent to decide what particular regulations they will
make for their own domestic government, as they
would be after the granting of the warrant; indeed,
it would seem that a very important part of their
preparation would be the formation of such a code,
to be submitted, with the petition for a warrant, as a
portion of the evidence of their capability in ·conducting the affairs of a lodge. If to this we add the
well-known rule, that even a warranted lodge must
submit its By-laws to the Grand Lodge for approval,
the argument in favor of our position would seem to
be complete. In like manner, we think that, if a
Lodge U. D. may initiate, pass and raise candidates,
and thus increase their numbers, they may with equal
propriety be intrusted with the power of affiliating
such Masons as they may deem worthy. Such is the
practice in the State of New York—these powers
being specifically conferred in the Dispensation,
which is granted to the persons named therein, and

not, like a warrant, to the first three officers. **No**
general law can, however, be stated, because Lodges
U. D., being a modern and almost exclusively American organization, each **Grand Lodge** makes such
regulations in regard to them as it may deem best
suited to the circumstances of its own jurisdiction.

SECTION II.—WARRANTED LODGES.

When the time fixed in the Dispensation has ex-
pired, the work of the Lodge ceases, and the next
step is the return of the Letters to the Grand Secretary, accompanied by a transcript of the minutes, a
copy of the By-laws, (where the Grand Lodge per-
mits Lodges U. D. to frame a code,) the proper Grand
Lodge return of work done, the constitutional fee,
and a petition for a warrant. These documents are
laid before the proper committee of the Grand Lodge,
and on their report the warrant issues.

A warrant once granted to a Lodge is immutable
so long as the Grand Lodge, of which it forms a constituent part, exists, and the members adhere to their
allegiance, and pay the contributions required by the
Constitution and Regulations of the Grand Lodge.
In this respect, it differs materially from the Dispensation ; for while the latter is an emanation from
the Grand Master, the Warrant has the direct sanction of the Grand Lodge, attested by its seal and

signatures—that is, those of the Grand Master, his Deputy, and the Grand Wardens—and can only be revoked by vote of the Grand Lodge, after due trial and unequivocal proof. The acts by which the warrant may be forfeited are—Contumacy to the authority of the Grand Master or Grand Lodge; Departure from the original plan of Masonry and Ancient Landmarks; Disobedience to the Constitutions; and Ceasing to meet for one year or more. The Warrant of a Lodge may be surrendered by the voluntary act of its members, after due summons, and when the minority opposed to such surrender is less than seven in number. It is proper to remark, that the majority of Masons agree with us in this opinion, and found it, as we do, upon the assumption, that as seven Master Masons are competent to form a Lodge, therefore, so long as that number remain faithful, and desire to retain the Warrant, it cannot be surrendered.*   A

* A remarkable confirmation of this view occurred not long since in New Orleans, where a majority of the members of a Lodge had formed themselves into an association, transferred to that association the property and funds, (a large amount,) and then declared the Lodge dissolved. The minority protesting against this action, a suit at law ensued; and it was finally decided by the Court of last resort, that the minority were the legal custodians of the Lodge and its properties, and that, although the majority might withdraw, they could not dissolve the Lodge, so long as a competent number of members were desirous of continuing its existence.

majority of the Grand Lodges hold to this view, and in England they require the minority to be less than three; but others, among which is the Grand Lodge of New York, allow a Warrant to be surrendered on the vote of a simple majority. As the Old Regulations make no mention of this occurrence in the history of a lodge, for the evident reason that previous to 1717 there were no Warrants to surrender, it is now conceded to be a subject of local regulation, and each Grand Lodge makes its own laws for its government.

The Warrant of a Lodge may be temporarily suspended, for cause, by the Grand Master; but such suspension cannot extend beyond the next ensuing Annual Communication of the Grand Lodge. In New York, this suspension carries with it that of all the members, unless they be specially exempted at the time, but this is clearly a local regulation,—the general understanding being that the Grand Master, by his edict, arrests the work of the Lodge, and prevents its meetings, but that the Warrant remains in force until lawfully revoked by the Grand Lodge.

But to return: The Warrant having been granted, it is necessary that certain ceremonies should be performed before the Lodge can be set at labor. These are :—

THE CONSECRATION, by which the Brethren composing the new Lodge are set apart to the work of ruling and governing the household intrusted to their care, for the "greater glory of God."

THE DEDICATION, by which they are reminded of the patrons of the Craft, and incited to emulate their virtues.

THE CONSTITUTION, by which, in the name and by authority of the Grand Lodge, they are formed into a just and regular assembly of Masons; and, finally,

THE INSTALLATION, by which the officers are inducted into their several stations, and formally invested with the powers thereunto belonging.

The order of these ceremonies, as here stated, differs somewhat from the general usage, but it is such as we have always practiced, and appears to be in keeping with the end sought to be obtained. These services should be performed by the Grand Master in person, or by his immediate delegate or proxy. It is admitted that no one but the Grand Master or his representative can Constitute a Lodge; and although the consecration and dedication are based upon the religious observances of antiquity, and are therefore religious in their nature, still they are essential to the legality of the whole ceremony; and while the Consecration Prayer ought to be rehearsed by the Chaplain, the formal declarations should all be made by the Grand Master.

4

When the ceremony is completed, the Lodge takes its place in the great Masonic family, as the peer of all other Lodges, as a constituent member of the Grand Lodge, by authority of which it has been ushered into existence, and at once enters into the enjoyment of all the rights, powers and privileges of a just and duly-constituted Lodge.

SECTION III.—POWERS OF WARRANTED LODGES.

The powers and privileges of a Subordinate or Particular Lodge are such as are defined in its warrant, by the Constitutions of the Grand Lodge granting the same, and the Ancient Landmarks and General Regulations. They are divided into—

1. EXECUTIVE : in the direction and performance of its work, under the control of its Master, and in all other matters in aid of the Master, who has the primary executive power of a Lodge.

2. LEGISLATIVE : embracing all matters relating to its internal concerns, not in derogation of the Ancient Landmarks, the Constitutions and General Regulations of the Grand Lodge, and its own particular By-laws; and,

3. JUDICIAL : embracing the exercise of discipline, and settlement of controversies between and over all its members (except the Master), and over all Masons

and non-affiliated brethren within its jurisdiction, subject to an appeal to the Grand Lodge.*

From what has already been said, it will be seen that, while in the beginning, Lodges were unrestricted by any superior authority, and were therefore supreme in themselves; yet, at the formation of Grand Lodges, certain of their powers were necessarily surrendered for the general good, just as individuals and communities divest themselves of a portion of their political rights, that all may enjoy a uniform protection at the hands of a supreme government. The idea of the surrender of a portion of their rights by the Lodges, carries with it the reservation of certain others, inherent in the Lodge, and not subject to dispensation or other act of the Grand Master or Grand Lodge. This is a most important distinction, and one that it is necessary to keep in remembrance in the decision of many of the questions that may be presented. The general tendency of all governments and legislative bodies is to cumulate power—to exercise not only the authority delegated to them by the people, but gradually to increase that authority by encroachments upon the original sovereignty. We believe in the simple doctrine that subordinate lodges are, as to many matters which have received the legislative

* Constitution, Grand Lodge of New York.

action of Grand Lodges, sovereign bodies, and that
any action which interferes with that sovereignty is
of necessity illegal and void; and that, unless the
reserved and inherent rights of Lodges are well defined and understood, the time will come when those
rights will be extinguished, partly through direct
legislation, and partly from the neglect, on the part
of the subordinates, to assert and maintain them.
The Lodge organization is the normal condition of
the Fraternity; Grand Lodges, the result of necessity, growing out of the wide-spread popularity and
extension of the institution, and intended to preserve
uniformity of doctrine and practice by mutual consultation on the part of the representatives of the
subordinate lodges. While each remains in its own
sphere of action, the result must continue to be in
the future, as it has been in the past, for the greatest
good of the Craft. Let it, however, be remembered
that the Grand Lodge acts by delegated powers, and
that, so far as those powers are concerned, it must
be supreme, but that the reserved powers of the
Lodge are inherent, and cannot be interfered with by
any act of the Grand Lodge; nay, more: we insist
that these powers cannot be delegated, if the Lodge
were so minded; for their possession by the subordinate body is a Landmark—a fundamental principle
—that no man or body of men can remove.

The powers of a Warranted Lodge may, therefore, be divided into two classes, INHERENT and CONSTITUTIONAL.

The inherent powers of a Lodge, controlled only by the Ancient Landmarks, are :—

1. To decide who shall be admitted members of or initiated therein; that is, of persons properly qualified.

2. To make Masons (not more than five at one meeting) of those it has decided to admit.

3. To place on trial a member against whom charges may have been preferred, to pronounce sentence, and enforce discipline.

4. To elect and install its officers.

5. To fix its time of meeting.

6. To require its members to contribute to its funds.

7. To be represented at all communications of the Grand Lodge.

8. To instruct its representatives, for their government, at all such communications of the Grand Lodge.

To our comprehension, these propositions are self-evident, and no lengthened commentary appears to be necessary. We direct attention to them, that it may be understood that no Grand Lodge legislation can alter their essential features. For example : it is usual and proper for Grand Lodges to fix, by con-stitutional provision, the time and manner of electing

officers; but, in the election, the Lodge is entirely
uncontrolled, save by its own By-laws and the usages
of Masonry. The Grand Lodge may say, that at a
given time a Lodge must elect a Master, two Wardens, a Treasurer, and a Secretary, but it cannot interfere with the choice by the brethren of persons to fill
those offices. So, the Grand Lodge may enact regulations for the government of Lodges in the trial of
members, but it cannot deprive the Lodge of its right
of original jurisdiction; it may, on appeal, reverse a
finding, and send the case back for a new trial, but
it cannot, in legal phraseology, change the venue, or
order the case to be tried elsewhere, without the consent of the Lodge. It cannot, by legislation, divest
the Masters and Wardens of the Warranted Lodges
in its jurisdiction of their right to represent their
Lodges, or of the Lodges to be represented by their
Masters and Wardens, in its annual or other communications, because to do so would be, in effect, to
destroy itself by destroying its members. Indeed,
the existence of this right is the very essence of
Grand Lodge organization, and carries with it the
right of instruction, to be exercised by the Lodges,
in their discretion.

The constitutional powers of a Lodge, subject to
control by the Grand Lodge, are :—

1. To make a code of By-laws for its internal gov-

ernment, not in derogation of its inalienable rights, or of those of its members.

2. To perform all the work pertaining to the three degrees of Ancient Craft Masonry.

3. To transact all business that can be legally transacted by a duly-constituted Lodge of Free-masons.

4. To appeal to the Grand Master or Grand Lodge from the decision of the presiding officer.

5. To change its place of meeting.

6. To control its funds.

It would seem as though the right to form and adopt a code of By-laws should be an exercise of original sovereignty, but when we reflect that these By-laws must be made to conform to the regulations of the Grand Lodge under the jurisdiction of which the Lodge works, we discover at once that this is a right given up for the general benefit to the control of the Grand Lodge, which right is, however, rarely or never exercised by the grand body beyond the supervision necessary to ascertain that the Lodge is neither depriving itself of its just rights, nor assuming powers and prerogatives that do not belong to it. A lodge may, therefore, enact a code of By-laws, change, amend, or repeal the same, in accordance with the provisions therein contained, and subject to the approval of the Grand Lodge, but for this reason it

cannot suspend them, because a suspension is in
reality an alteration or amendment, which is not valid
without the approval of the Grand Lodge : hence, a
motion to suspend a by-law is not in order. And,
again, it might be asked, that if the Lodge has an
inalienable right to make Masons, why it has not
unlimited control over the work? The reason is,
that the Grand Lodge, by the very nature of the case,
must have superintendence of the work and lectures,
in order to guard against the introduction of matters
foreign to the original idea of Masonry, to prevent
the inexperienced and the over-zealous from *embel-
lishing* the ritual, which, if allowed to have their own
way, they would do, and that to such an extent, that
the original form would disappear. It is evident that
the Grand Lodge, composed as it is of all the Masters
and Wardens in its jurisdiction, can better maintain
and preserve the ritual from innovation, than any
single lodge could do, however well the lodge might
be disposed. Moreover, lodges in the beginning only
conferred the first, or Entered Apprentice degree ;
the control of the ritual has, therefore, never been
left entirely to their discretion.

For similar reasons the business of the Lodge, as
contra-distinguished from the ritualistic ceremonies,
is necessarily subject to the supervision and control
of the Grand Lodge. The retention of this right by

the Grand Lodge is, if we may so term it, a portion of the contract, by which that body ceded to the subordinates the right to confer the second and third degrees; and this is why it is now held that Master Masons only can be members of a lodge, and that hence all the business of a lodge must be transacted in the third degree. The examination of candidates for advancement, and the trial of Entered Apprentices and Fellow Crafts (see TRIALS) will necessarily form exceptions.

The appeal to the Grand Lodge from the decision of the Master, or of the Warden presiding in his absence, is evidently of no older date than the creation of the appellate body, and must, therefore, be governed by the General Regulations. Fortunately, for the well-being and good discipline of the Fraternity, it is a right that is so seldom exercised, that it is only necessary to name its existence to have said all that is required on the subject.

When Lodges met by authority of the civil magistrates, they of course fixed their own time and place of meeting; and as one meeting had no positive relation to those preceding or succeeding it, the convenience of the brethren was the only governing rule; but when Lodges came to meet under sanction of a Warrant, and thus entered upon a continued existence, it became necessary that they should have a fixed locality, to prevent confusion among the lodges themselves, and to enable the Grand Lodge to know where to find its constituents; hence the rule, that while a lodge, after due summons and vote of its members, may change its place of meeting from one locality to another, in the same city, town or village, it cannot remove from one city, town or village to another, without the sanction of the Grand Lodge.

The lodge treasury, like the individual pocket, is extremely sensitive to interference, and Grand Lodges have wisely abstained from any attempt to exercise control over the funds of their subordinates, beyond requiring that they shall not be recklessly squandered, or divided among the members, while the just debts of the lodge remain unpaid, or while the Grand Lodge dues are unprovided for; but, these things taken care of, it has been decided that a lodge may appropriate its funds to a worthy object, even though it be not a strictly Masonic one.

SECTION IV.—PRECEDENCY AND JURISDICTION OF LODGES.

Lodges take precedence according to the seniority of their respective warrants—that is, Lodge No. 1 is necessarily of older date than Lodge No. 300, and, so far as the respect due to age and services goes, is entitled to all the consideration that may justly be accorded to age and long service.   The senior lodges are also entitled, by their representatives, to fill temporarily any vacancies in the stations that may occur at a meeting of the Grand Lodge, and to take, according to number, the right of Masonic processions; but beyond these comparatively unimportant privileges, there is no difference between the *status* of the oldest or youngest Lodge, except what each one may create for itself by attention to the Constitution and Regulations, the general usages of Masonry, and a proper attention to the selection of *materiel* and the rights of its peers.

The jurisdiction of Lodges is of two kinds—TERRITORIAL and PENAL:

The territorial jurisdiction of a Lodge depends entirely upon the regulations enacted by the Grand Lodge to which it owes allegiance, and may be stated, in general terms, to extend half-way in every direction to the nearest Lodge within the territorial jurisdiction of the Grand Lodge. In cities and towns where there are two or more lodges, their jurisdiction is held to be in all respects concurrent. Jurisdiction, as here defined, relates entirely to the reception of profanes; for a Lodge retains jurisdiction over its members, without regard to their place of residence. This is another law growing out of the increase of Lodges, and is intended, by securing to each one a well-defined limit in which to seek for material, to enable it to make a more thorough investigation into the character and standing of candidates, than it could otherwise do, and, by preventing trespass on the territory of its neighbors, to insure a greater degree of harmony. This rule may, at first sight, appear to interfere with the right of Lodges to decide who shall be initiated therein, and to make Masons of those they have thus decided to admit; but a lodge can only entertain the petition of, or confer degrees on, a properly-qualified candidate; and it is now held (except by the Grand Lodges of England and Hamburg) that a candidate is not properly qualified unless he has a fixed residence within the territorial jurisdiction of the Lodge to which he applies. Seafaring men, and military and naval officers, are excepted from this rule, because they are supposed, from the nature of their professions, not to be able to control their private actions so far as to be in any place long enough, at one time, to establish a residence, in the legal acceptation of the term. Master Masons are excepted from this rule, because they have acquired all the rights and privileges of the Craft—one of which is, that every Mason may choose for himself the Lodge in which he can best work, and with the members of which he can best agree.

The penal jurisdiction of a Lodge, by which is understood the right of trial and the enforcement of discipline, other than that exercised over its own members, (to which we shall give a separate consideration,) extends to all non-affiliated Masons in its jurisdiction, and to Masons belonging to lodges located in other jurisdictions, but who are personally within the jurisdiction of the disciplining lodge. This is a law of common justice, as well as one of ancient usage, but not of universal acceptance,— many authorities claiming that if a member of a lodge in Minnesota commit a Masonic offence in Vermont, he can only be tried by his mother-lodge; but it is evident that the offender in Vermont might go on to any excess, and by his conduct bring unutterable shame on the lodge and brethren for any length of time, before the lodge in Minnesota could be informed of it, or, if informed, could obtain the evidence necessary to a conviction; while, on the other hand, the lodge in Vermont, in whose very presence the offence might be said to be committed, would certainly be best prepared to administer correction with a knowledge of the facts. Every Lodge and every Mason is bound to maintain to the utmost the good name and reputation of the Fraternity, and to this end all regular lodges are justified in summoning before them, for trial, those non-affiliated Masons and members of distant lodges who, forgetful of the solemn sanctions under which they entered the Craft, violate its wholesome regulations, and thus bring disgrace upon it. The principle upon which this law is founded is coeval with the organization of Masonry as we have it. It is not only a Landmark in itself, but a necessary sequence of other principles about which there is no difference of opinion; thus, a Mason is required to be a peaceable citizen, wherever he resides or works, by which is understood that he is to conform to the law, respect the magistrates, and act as a good citizen should do, that the honor of the Fraternity may be thereby promoted, and the cavils of its adversaries answered. Now, if a Mason is thus required to demean himself in regard to the civil law, how can he be exempted from like provisions in the code of Masonry? Lodges are but the subdivisions of a universal family, for the convenience of the brethren; the general reputation and prosperity of the whole is, therefore, of greater importance than the mere local interests or pride of a small part, and every Lodge is consequently a guardian—so to speak—of the general good name, with undoubted right, in the execution of its trust, to summon before it delinquent sojourners and non-affiliated Masons, to place them on trial, and after lawful conviction to administer discipline; subject, it need hardly be said, to an appeal to the Grand Lodge to which the disciplining lodge owes obedience.

CHAPTER IV.

The Officers of a Lodge.

SECTION I.—THEIR POWERS AND DUTIES.

HAVING thus far treated of the general powers of
a Lodge, it is necessary to our plan that we should
now introduce the officers, as a knowledge of their
powers and duties is essential to a proper understanding of various matters that will appear as we
proceed.

The discipline of a Masonic Lodge, the order observed at its meetings, the obedience there exacted,
and cheerfully rendered on the part of the brethren,
makes its government as nearly perfect as it is possible for any merely human institution to be. It
should, therefore, be—as in truth it generally is—a
matter of study and just pride, on the part of the
office-bearers, to be well acquainted with the general
laws and usages of the society, as well as with their
own powers, prerogatives and duties, that not only
may they be enabled to keep the members in the
straight path of duty, but that, by their own example,
they may make that path more easily discernible,
and less apt to be departed from. Intelligent and

capable officers make good Lodges, and govern with less difficulty than ignorant and incompetent ones, because they do not overstep the bounds of propriety, nor heedlessly invade the rights of the brethren; and because all men—certainly all men fit to be Masons—appreciate the labors of such officers, and intuitively seek to assist them by prompt deference to their commands, and the influence which such conduct exercises over those—if any there be—less loyally inclined.

The duties and prerogatives of the officers are always well defined, but it is none the less a fact that, in scarcely any two rites, are the officers and their functions precisely the same, and, indeed, our own country is not entirely uniform, although all Lodges in the United States work under the supervision of Grand Lodges of what is termed the *Ancient York Rite*.* In some jurisdictions, they have an

---

* We may be deemed heretical, but we cannot avoid saying, that, in our judgment, the name of *York Rite*, as applied to our system of degrees, is an absolute misnomer. Every ritualist who has investigated the subject knows, that the simplicity of the Ancient System has been buried, as it were, under the innovations of WEBB and his successors in the business of ritual-making; that we have, in fact, a system peculiar to ourselves, which we ought to call, what it really is, "*The American Rite.*" The reader will, of course, make the distinction between those who seek to create new rituals, and those who faithfully and earnestly teach what they have previously learned.

officer called the *Inner Guard;* in others, such an officer is unknown: some have *Masters of Ceremonies;* others, not. In the beginning, the indispensable officers were the *Master, Wardens* and *Tiler.* The creation of new rites and other causes have, however, gradually led to the introduction of other officials, and a Lodge may now be said to be fully officered when it has—

> A MASTER, (whose style is *Worshipful,*)
> A SENIOR WARDEN,
> A JUNIOR WARDEN,
> A TREASURER,
> A SECRETARY,
> A SENIOR DEACON,
> A JUNIOR DEACON,
> Two STEWARDS, or
> Two MASTERS OF CEREMONIES,
> A TILER.

In addition to these, many Lodges have a CHAPLAIN, some a PHYSICIAN, others a MARSHAL, and most, if not all, a BOARD OF TRUSTEES.

THE MASTER.

"It was the observation of a wisdom greater than man can boast, that a house or kingdom divided against itself, cannot stand; and experience proves the soundness of the axiom. This proverb may be applied with great propriety to an institution whose members are segregated from the rest of the world by obligations, customs, and laws of a peculiar nature, yet retain their independence of character by a perfect freedom of thought and action. In such a society, a judicious ruler is absolutely essential, not merely to its prosperity, but to its very existence. If the shepherd be careless or inefficient, the flock will be scattered abroad.

"Unity is the mainspring of Freemasonry. Destroy that, and the machinery will fall in pieces; and it will be a difficult matter to preserve the links in the chain of unity unbroken, unless the Master pursue an accommodating policy, which may cause the brethren to be mutually pleased with each other's society, accompanied by an inflexible regard to discipline, which, while it allows freedom of action, will preserve inviolable the respectful submission that is due the Chair, as its undoubted and inalienable prerogative."*

"To become Master of his Lodge, is the legitimate object of every young brother who takes any interest in our society. The very questionable policy of our present regulations seems to be, to open to each, in succession, the way to the Mastership—almost, if not altogether, as a matter of course. Now, my younger brethren may rest assured, that although, in deference to a usage which it is perhaps too late to abolish, we may place a careless or ignorant Mason in the Chair, invest him with the badge of authority, and address him with the external forms of respect, we cannot command for him the deference and consideration which will be sure to follow the enlightened and expert. He will be like the figure-

---

* "Revelations of a Square."—OLIVER.

head of a ship—placed foremost, and gaudily decorated; but, after all, it is a mere effigy, not contributing in the least to the management of the vessel. In small, as in great things, *knowledge* is power—*intellectual superiority* is real pre-eminence."

" Some inexperienced brethren may think that no difficulty can ever arise in the decision of Masonic questions, because they have never seen any such difficulty in our society. It is true, that mutual forbearance is so much inculcated, and good feeling so widely prevails among us, that, in the hands of a judicious ruler, all goes on with easy and undeviating regularity. But I can assure them that, in a well-regulated Lodge, there is a very ample scope for the exercise of intellect; and that the Master will soon find that he requires even more than a knowledge of Masonic law and usages, to acquit himself creditably of his responsibility. He should know his own limits, so as not to encroach upon the rights of the brethren, of which, I candidly warn every young Master, he will find us not a little jealous. If he falls short of his own bounds, or oversteps them, he will find clear heads and keen tongues to remind him—respectfully, but unmistakably—of the fact. The Lodge will soon feel what sort of hand holds the helm; and as they are bound to acquiesce in his opinion, as their Master, he must show equal deference to theirs."*

"In the whole series of offices recognized by the Masonic institution, there is not one more important than that of the

* "The Duty of the Master," a Lecture, by J. Fitz-Henry Townsend.—*American Quarterly Review of Freemasonry*, vol. i.

Master of a Lodge. Upon the skill, integrity and prudence of the presiding officer, depend the usefulness and welfare of the Lodge, and as lodges are the primary assemblages of the Craft, and by representation constitute the supreme tribunal or Grand Lodge, it is evident that the errors of government in the primary bodies must, if not duly corrected, be productive of evil to the whole fraternity. Hence, in the ceremony of Installation, it was required, as a necessary qualification of him who was proposed to the Grand Master as the presiding officer of a Lodge, that he should be of good morals, of great skill, true and trusty, and a lover of the whole fraternity, wheresoever dispersed over the face of the earth. And it was on such a recommendation, that it was to be presumed that he would discharge the duties of the office with fidelity."*

To the foregoing qualifications of the Master, which are general in their nature, there is to be added the legal one, that he shall have previously been installed and served as Warden—not necessarily in the Lodge which proposes to elect him, but, at all events, in some regular Lodge. As considerable difference of opinion exists in regard to this question, we propose to give it a brief examination. The original law upon the subject is found in the fourth of the Ancient Charges. In this Charge it is stated, "That all preferment among Masons is grounded upon real worth

"Text-book of Masonic Jurisprudence."—MACKEY.

and personal merit only;" that "none but a perfect youth should be made an Apprentice, that in due time he may become a Fellow Craft, and when otherwise qualified, arrive at the honor of being Warden, and then Master of the Lodge." * * * * "No brother can be a Warden until he has passed the part of a Fellow Craft; nor a Master till he has acted as Warden."—To our comprehension, and, we may add, to that of a large majority of the Fraternity, this law is so explicit, as not to admit of any fair argument against the requirement which so plainly appears in its language—that a brother must be a Warden before he can be Master. We have seen much ingenious argument to prove that, as all preferment among Masons depends on personal merit, such merit must be the governing rule in the selection of the Master, as well as other officers; but it will be seen that "real worth and personal merit" are the groundwork only of preferment, and they neither include nor, by a reasonable deduction, forbid the necessity of other qualifications. As a basis of preferment, we cheerfully acknowledge personal merit to be indispensable, and regard it as one of the most satisfactory features of the Masonic institution—as one that especially distinguishes it from the associations of the profane world; but to make this the only test, would be to sweep away, as with a breath, other distinguishing

and valuable characteristics of the Fraternity. If
the personally meritorious were all eligible to the
mastership, the Master Mason of a day might aspire
to the chief command, as well as the veteran of half
a century, and thus our lodges would become so many
arenas for the exhibition of the chicanery and tricks
of partisan politics, while the experience and education necessary to fit even the truly meritorious for so
difficult a trust as that of Master of a Lodge, would
at once be left out of the account. Fortunately, for
the stability of the Craft, the advocates of such a
theory are few and far between. The Charge itself
is the best refutation, if any were needed, of the argument under consideration; for it plainly contemplates
the gradual arrival of the aspirant to the goal of his
ambition :—the Apprentice is to become a Fellow
Craft in due time, and when he has served such a
term of years as the custom of the country directs,
and is *otherwise qualified*, he may arrive to the honor
of being Warden, *and then* Master. In the words
"otherwise qualified," something beside "personal
merit" is clearly provided for and intended.

There is another, and somewhat more numerous,
class, who claim that, under certain circumstances, a
Lodge may proceed to elect to the mastership any
member of the Lodge, even though he may never
have been Warden. We have seen a report, adopted

by a Grand Lodge, in which it is gravely argued that "acting as Warden" is merely a ceremonial observance, and has no further effect than to require that the candidate should have temporarily occupied the Warden's station during the conferring of a degree. We cannot fully expose the fallacy of this position without trenching on matters not proper to be written; but every Master Mason knows, or ought to know, that there were three Grand Masters, neither of whom was Warden—the duties of that station being confided to the "Overseers of the work," and, therefore, that the ceremony referred to is without the quality of common sense. "Acting as Warden" means to have been lawfully appointed to that station, and to have discharged the duties that pertain to it.

In ANDERSON'S second edition of the Constitutions, published in 1738, he makes two very important changes in the Regulation in regard to the qualifications of the Master. The first is simply explanatory, by the addition of the word "somewhere;" that is, that a brother should have been Warden somewhere, but not necessarily in the Lodge in which he was to be elected Master. The second overthrows the whole, by the addition of these words: "except in extraordinary cases, or when a Lodge is to be formed where none such (Past Masters or Wardens) can be had; for then three Master Masons, though never Masters

or Wardens of Lodges before, may be constituted
Master and Wardens of that new Lodge." If, as
stated in the title, the Constitutions of 1721 were the
"Laws, Charges, Orders, Regulations and Usages of
the Right Worshipful Fraternity of Accepted Freemasons," and were collected "from their general
records and their faithful traditions of many ages,"
then he had no authority whatever to alter them in
1738, nor could the Grand Lodge of England, if they
had been faithful to their trust, have sanctioned any
such alteration. The Constitutions of 1721 were
either correct or they were not : if correct, they were
the usages of "many ages;" and that they were so,
seems to follow from the fact of their approval and
authorized publication by the Grand Lodge. And,
although it is provided, in the thirty-ninth General
Regulation, "that every Annual Grand Lodge has
inherent power and authority to make *new regulations*
or to alter these, for the real benefit of this Ancient
Fraternity," it is clear that this only refers to local
regulations; for it is expressly declared that such
new regulations can only be made or the old ones
changed on condition "*that the old landmarks be carefully preserved.*" The requirement that a Master
must previously have been a Warden, we are told
was the usage of many ages, and the conclusion is
irresistible that there was no power in any body of

men to make an innovation by changing it. "But" —we shall here be told—" you admit that any Master Mason may be appointed Master of a new Lodge, or, as we have it, a Lodge under Dispensation." We admit the fact, but we deny the principle, for one proposition carries the other with it; and if the Grand Master can, under the regulations of his Grand Lodge, appoint any member to be Master of a new Lodge, by the same authority he might grant his Dispensation to elect a member from the floor of a Warranted Lodge, and thus the English practice of removing a landmark would be fully established. If, however, we admit that the Grand Lodge of England had power to change the Regulation of 1721, in regard to the qualifications of Masters, then we must also grant to every other Grand Lodge a similar authority, and thus make the subject one of local legislation. Such is, indeed, its present condition. The right of the Grand Master to appoint any Master Mason to the mastership of a Lodge under Dispensation is universally conceded. The Grand Lodge of New York makes this exception, but otherwise maintains the rule in its ancient form. Section 38 of its Constitution is in these words :—"No member can be Master of a Lodge, unless he has been previously installed, and served as an elected Warden for one year, except at the institution of a new Lodge, when

5

no Warden or Past Master is found to serve as Master." With one or two exceptions, we believe, every Grand Lodge in the United States has a similar provision in its Constitution; and while, therefore, the principle remains as we have stated it, the practice must be governed by the regulations of the Grand Lodge having jurisdiction.

We now pass to the consideration of the prerogatives of the Master, which are :—

1. *The right to congregate his Lodge.*—The law for this is found in the second of the Regulations of 1721, but some explanation seems to be necessary to its proper understanding. There are two meanings attached to the word *congregate,* one of which is the ordinary acceptation, meaning the calling together of the brethren, at a time and place named, for the purpose of holding a meeting; and the other, the Masonic one, referring to the ceremony by which the Master calls the brethren to order, when so assembled, for the purpose of setting them at labor in a formed lodge. It is an immemorial usage—and, therefore, a landmark—that none but the Master (when he is present) can congregate the brethren,* although the formal ceremony of opening may be performed by another brother in his presence and under his direction. Under this prerogative, the

---

* In the second sense of the word. See Prerogative 9.

Master may call or summon a meeting of his lodge at any time he thinks proper; but, though in former times he could call it at any time or *place*, his power in this respect is now restricted, under the regulations of Grand Lodges, to the calling of special communications at the place usually occupied by the Lodge; at which special communications no business can be transacted, save that for which the meeting is called; and, further, that no business relative to the presentation of petitions for initiations or adjoining, or a ballot on such petitions, can be had at a called meeting. The stated communications are fixed by the Lodge itself, as well as the place where they are to be held; and though the Master may, if he please, summon the members for any meeting, he cannot alter the time or place of the stated ones, because he has agreed to observe the By-laws, and to stand to the awards of the brethren, so far as they do not interfere with his admitted prerogatives.

2. *The right to preside.*—This is a self-evident proposition, and follows as a natural consequence of his installation: but there is this peculiarity attaching to the Master of a Masonic Lodge, viz: that once duly installed, he cannot during his term of office be deprived of his right to preside by any power residing in the Lodge itself. By the terms of his covenant at installation, he is bound "to pay homage to the

Grand Master for the time being, and to his officers,
when duly installed :" hence, when the Grand Master
or his Deputy, or other duly-appointed representative, appears in a Lodge, the power of the Master to
preside temporarily disappears, unless the superior
authority waive the right thus vesting in him, a courtesy which, it is perhaps needless to say, is almost
universally exercised. From this right of the Master
ensue others, intimately connected with it, as

3. *The right to fill, temporarily, any vacancies that
may occur in the Lodge Offices.*—It is his duty to set
the Craft at labor, and, in order to do so, he needs
the active coöperation of all the other officers; and
it is, therefore, necessary to the proper execution of
his trust that he should have full power to select from
the brethren present such as he deems competent to
discharge the functions of the absent incumbents.

4. *To control the admission of visitors.*—It is, beyond question, that one of the most important duties
of a faithful Master is the preservation of harmony
among the brethren by the exercise of sleepless vigilance against the admission of cowans, or of those
brethren who, if admitted, would by their presence
disturb the peace of the Lodge and hinder its work.
In the exercise of this right, therefore, the Master
may refuse admission to any visitor, however correct
the standing of the visitor may be, he being respon-

sible for the exercise of his prerogative. For a similar reason, it is the general practice of the Master—
though not absolutely bound to do so—to refuse a
visitor when any member of the Lodge objects to his
visit. It is held that he may even go farther, and
refuse a member of his own Lodge, subject of course
to the penalties that would follow an abuse of that
power. As an abstract proposition, this is probably
correct; yet it is hedged round with so many difficulties, and treads so close upon the right accorded
to every member in good standing, to participate in
the work of his Lodge, that we cannot but advise
that it should never be exercised, or, at least, only in
such flagrant cases as would demand a similar action
on the part of the Lodge, if the power were not
already vested in the Master. We are all liable to
error, and but few men are exempt from the influence
of a momentary pique, or the impulse of sudden passion. At such a time, the compasses lose their power,
and we become liable to do that which, in our cooler
moments, we might sincerely regret. It should also
be remembered that a member so refused, has an
appeal to the Grand Master or Grand Lodge, and,
if unjustly dealt with, may even prefer charges; in
which case, the trouble ensuing would more than
counterbalance any good expected to result from the
exclusion.

5. *To regulate and terminate all discussion.*—The distinction between the Master of a Masonic Lodge and the presiding officer of any other association, is no where more strikingly exemplified than in the exercise of this prerogative. While, in other societies, the president—or whatever title he may assume—presides, in our Lodges, the Master *rules and governs.* In the execution of his trust, he wields autocratic powers, and, for the time being, the Lodge must obey. Hence, when in his judgment the debate has extended far enough, or when it is degenerating into criminations and personalities—as unfortunately will sometimes occur—he rises in his place, and the floor is his; he proceeds to put the question, if a question be pending, or to direct the labors in some other channel.

6. *To direct the order of business.*—It has become a custom, of late years, for lodges to append to their By-laws a summary of the order in which business shall be transacted at the stated communications, and Masters are gradually falling into the habit of its use, on the ground of convenience. It is very distinctly within our recollection when no such thing was known—at least, not to our knowledge—and we have always protested against it during the years of our mastership by paying no attention to any such rules. If a Master is competent to fill the station he

occupies, he ought to be, and is, the best judge of what to do and when to do it. Every Master should assert this power, as a standing protest against the innovations which are gradually, but surely, making their way among us.

7. *To appoint all Committees.*—Being responsible for the proper conduct of the affairs of the Lodge, it is but just that the Master should have the selection of the committees. If such were not the case, the Master would, to that extent, be under the direction of the Lodge, a position in which he can never be lawfully placed. The Master is considered, by virtue of his office, a member of all committees, and when he chooses to attend their deliberations, the deference due to his position makes him Chairman. The right is, however, seldom exercised, and in some cases—as the committee to try charges against a brother—ought not to be at all. He has also generally the appointment of such of the subordinate officers as are not elected under the By-laws; this, however, is not an irrevocable right, for the custom has varied at different periods and in different jurisdictions. Thus, in England, he appoints the Wardens, and they in turn appoint officers of lower grade than themselves; in some jurisdictions, the Lodge elects all the officers; in others, the Master appoints all below the Secretary.

8. *To close the Lodge at will.*—By this it is not

assumed that the Master may close his Lodge in the midst of its labors at the mere suggestion of his own arbitrary will, for that would be intolerable; but that he is the proper judge as to when the labors ought reasonably to cease, and the brethren retire to their several homes. Perhaps no single objection against Masonic Lodges has been urged with greater force than that which has for its theme the detention of the brethren to an unreasonable hour of the night. The world is all too apt to believe whatever may be stated to the prejudice of our society, and it would be difficult to furnish an argument likely to be more industriously used against us, than the unfortunate habit many lodges have contracted of protracting their meetings to unreasonable hours. Married men owe it to their families, and single ones to their reputations, to be at home before midnight; and it is well that Masters should recollect their prerogative, and exercise it by closing their Lodges at such an hour as will enable the brethren to be at home in good season. Cases may arise, in which it is the bounden duty of the Master to close his Lodge summarily, and in such an event, there is no question as to his authority so to do. In all well-governed Lodges, however, the occurrence of such a scene would be next to an impossibility.

It has been, and is still held to be, a prerogative

of the Master to open his Lodge at the hour he thinks appropriate ; but while we do not dispute the fact, we think he may be safely admitted to have waived this in favor of the Lodge, to secure the attendance of the brethren at a fixed time, in order that all may know what to depend upon ; and that no unfair advantage may be taken of the presence of certain brethren, or the absence of others, to bring forward or keep back a favorite measure.

9. *To issue summons.*—We have already alluded to this power in the first-mentioned prerogative of the Master, but only as to meetings, the topic then under consideration. He has, however, power to summon for various purposes, in addition to meetings : as, witnesses in trials ; all Masons within the jurisdiction of his Lodge, to answer complaints against them ; the officers of his Lodge, to render their accounts or to answer for delinquencies ; the members of his Lodge, to attend the funeral of a deceased brother. The summons can be issued by authority of the Master only, while he remains in the discharge of his functions, and is a peremptory order, which must be obeyed, under penalty, unless the excuse of the defaulter be of the most undeniable validity. A summons is usually in writing, signed by the Master, countersigned by the Secretary, and having the Lodge seal attached ; but there is no doubt that a verbal

summons by the Master is equally binding with a written one.

10. *To be the custodian of the Warrant.*— Although the Warrant purports on its face to be granted to the Master and Wardens, yet, at his installation, it is placed in special charge of the Master, and he is made responsible for its safe keeping. As, under the present organization of the Fraternity, no Lodge can be established without a Warrant, and as its presence is necessary to the legality of all meetings, it follows that the powers of the Master can only be exercised under its sanction ; and it is, therefore, but just that he should, at all times, be in possession of the evidence of his authority. There is, in many cases, a want of care, on the part of Masters, in regard to this important document. We have frequently seen it framed, and hung up in the Lodge-room ; in other cases, we have known it to be regularly committed to the keeping of the Tiler at the close of the meeting, and sometimes it is put away in a package with the Secretary's books—all of which practices appear to us extremely reprehensible. It is delivered to the Master in person, and it ought to remain in his personal custody. It is true, that even then an accident might happen ; but, in that event, there would remain the satisfaction of knowing that the duty of personal care had been fully discharged. In

case of loss of the Warrant—by fire, for instance—it is a simple matter for the Grand Lodge to issue a new one, equally valid, in a legal point of view, with the original, but it would only be a duplicate; and when, as is not uncommon, all the original signers have passed away, the loss is irreparable, nor will the regret attending it be lessened by the reflection that carelessness may be cited as its moving cause.

Under certain circumstances, the custody of the Warrant passes to the Wardens, as will be seen when we come to speak of those officers.

11. *In company with the Senior and Junior Wardens, to represent his Lodge at all communications of the Grand Lodge.*—While it must be admitted that this is a right, which came into existence at the establishment of a Grand Lodge, after the revival of Masonry in 1717, it is none the less, now, inalienable. We see in the Regulations of 1721 that it is provided, that "the Grand Lodge consists of, and is formed by, the Master and Wardens of all the regular particular Lodges upon record." And, again, "the majority of every particular Lodge, when congregated, shall have the privilege of giving instructions to their Master and Wardens before the assembling of the Grand Lodge— * * * * * because their Master and Wardens are their representatives, and are supposed to speak their mind." From this it follows, that with-

out the representatives of the subordinate or particular Lodges, there is no Grand Lodge; and as no legislation can be effected without their consent, it is not to be supposed they will disfranchise themselves. By the terms of his installation, and as the executive of the Lodge will, the Master is especially charged with the duty of representation.

In the exercise of these prerogatives, other and correlative exhibitions of authority are sometimes called forth; as

The control of the minutes, so far as to see that nothing improper to be written is recorded; and, on the other hand, that nothing essential to a fair record of the proceedings is omitted.

The right to refuse to initiate a candidate, notwithstanding his acceptance by the Lodge, if, in his judgment, such initiation would be improper.

The right, when the first ballot for a candidate appears to be unfavorable, to order a second—he taking care that the necessary cautions be observed, and that the re-balloting be done before any brother participating in the first ballot has left the Lodge.

The right to discuss all questions, without regard to the parliamentary etiquette of leaving the Chair, because it is his duty, at all times, to give the Craft good and wholesome instruction; in any remarks, therefore, which he may be pleased to make, he is presumed to act for the best interests of the brethren.

He signs all drafts upon the Treasurer, without which, that officer would not be justified in paying out the Lodge funds.

He is exempt from trial by the Lodge. This proposition is a legitimate sequence of his official prerogatives. We have seen that he has the right to preside at all times, and to decide, without the possibility of an appeal being taken from his decision to that of the Lodge. If, therefore, a motion should be offered to put him on trial, he might refuse to entertain it; and, even worse, he might, if his trial were allowed in the Lodge, be called to sit as judge in his own case; for the Lodge cannot deprive him of his right to preside. He has the right to appoint all committees: in selecting one before which his trial should be had, (where that mode of trial is adopted,) he would, of course, select his personal friends, and use his influence with them to secure an acquittal. It is, therefore, held that some tribunal, other than the Lodge, shall be charged with the trial of the Master, and that tribunal is, by universal consent, the Grand Lodge.

He is entitled, and required to receive the degree of Past Master previous to his installation, because it is an indispensable part of that ceremony; without the possession of which he could not lawfully preside, and by which he is furnished with instruction for his guidance while occupying the Chair.

He cannot dimit or resign during his term of office, because he has entered into a solemn covenant to discharge the duties of Master for one year from the time of his election, which is in itself a promise that he will not resign. If he cannot resign, he cannot dimit; because, if allowed to withdraw, he might affiliate with another Lodge, and thus be Master of one while a member of another, an argument which requires no refutation.

No vacancy can occur in his office, except by death or expulsion. The Constitution of New York provides another cause, by "removal beyond the jurisdiction," which, with all deference to our mother Grand Lodge, we think untenable, for this reason:— It is universally conceded that a Master Mason ought to belong to a Lodge, and that it is his right to affiliate with the one that suits him, without regard to its location or his residence; or, to make the matter plainer, that a Master Mason residing in New Orleans, may, if he choose, affiliate with a Lodge in Boston, if the Lodge think proper to affiliate him. This being true, it follows that removal beyond the jurisdiction does not affect the membership of the Master; and while he continues a member in good standing, his right to the office in which he has been installed remains indefeasible.

Where a vacancy actually occurs by death or expulsion, it is generally held that the Grand Master may issue his dispensation, authorizing a new election to fill the vacancy thus created. From this proposition we also dissent, because it is the admitted prerogative of the Senior Warden, in the event of such vacancy, to succeed to the Chair, and, in his absence, the Junior Warden succeeds by immemorial right—a right which even the edict of the Grand Master cannot abrogate. If, however, all three offices are vacant, it would then be proper to hold a new election, under authority of the Grand Master, but not otherwise.

The conclusion to which the young Mason, after reading this summary of the powers of the Master, will naturally arrive is, that he is a perfect despot; and so, in one sense, he is—in the Lodge. But the masonic system is amply provided with what, in diplomatic language, are called "checks and balances;" and for every power intrusted to and exercised by the Master, there is a corresponding responsibility. If he err—as Masters, being but men, will sometimes do—there is the superior power of the Grand Master to correct his error, and restore the *status quo*. His powers are a peculiarity of the institution, and cannot be changed without altering its entire character, which no one can do, if any were so inclined. Among us the possession of these powers seems to render the heedless careful, and the careful, conservative; and while the brethren render due obedience, carefully observing the statutes and regulations, there is nothing to fear from the exercise of arbitrary powers on the part of the Master. Finally, to again quote Brother TOWNSEND, "We have seen that the brethren must, in all lawful things, obey their Master. He, on his part, should have no object but the advantage, welfare and comfort of his brethren. We may teach him our forms, explain to him their meaning, stimulate his ambition to discharge his duties creditably; but, after all, we must leave him to look within his own heart for instruction, and to be guided by his own good sense and good feeling in his general conduct. But, although particular rules will not avail to supply the want of good sense and discretion, yet there are two general maxims, of which the Master should never lose sight:—First, to be *serious;* secondly, to be *strict* in observing what are called the Landmarks of the Craft."

PAST MASTER.

Though perhaps somewhat in the nature of an interpolation, this appears to be the proper place to call attention to the *status* of Past Masters. It has been well said, that "Past officers have no powers as such, except the respect due to their standing, skill and experience, save what is expressly given them by the Constitutions of their Grand Lodges,"—although it is but partially true. When a Master has arrived at the end of his official term, and has installed his successor, he loses all the rights which, as an actual Master, he had been exercising, and becomes again the peer of the brethren, subject, like them, to be ruled and governed by the new Master; but by the very fact of having been installed, and having served as Master, certain privileges inure to him, which are not possessed by any brother who has not attained to that rank. Thus, in the fourth of the Ancient Charges, it is provided that "no brother can be a Grand Warden till he has been Master of a Lodge;" and that "the Grand Master has power to choose his Deputy, who must be then, or must have been, the Master of a particular Lodge." The Grand Master himself is only required to have been a Fellow Craft; but in the many changes which these Charges have since undergone, it has come to be required that the Grand Master also shall have been Master of a Lodge. It is clear that, under the present regulations of the Fraternity, he must be at least a *Master Mason;* but we do not hazard anything in saying, that no Grand Lodge would now elect a Grand Master who had not previously acquired the experience of at least one term as Master of a Lodge. Therefore, we say that it is a privilege of a Past Master to be eligible to office in the Grand Lodge. In all Grand Lodges it is the rule that Lodges may be represented by proxy when the actual officers are absent: in about half of them, any Master Mason in good standing, and a member of the Lodge he represents, can be such proxy; in the others, he is required to be a Past Master. As a general rule, we think that in all cases a Past Master would have the preference.

A Past Master is qualified to install any *Master elect*, when requested to do so, and to be present at the qualification of a Master elected to the Chair for the first time.* We may here digress a moment, to say that, although some authorities declare that a virtual or Chapter Past Master may be present, and assist at such qualification, we entirely dissent from the assertion. The degree of Past Master, as conferred in a Chapter, is a prerequisite to the reception of the next higher grade, and can only be conferred on those who have received the preceding or *Mark Master's degree*, a qualification not necessarily possessed by the Master elect, who is about to be qualified for installation, by the reception of the *Past Master's degree*. In one case, it is merely a ceremonial

* See ELECTIONS.

qualification for a higher degree ; in the other, it is part of the installation, by which the Master is invested with power to govern an actual Lodge. Again, it is the year of service in the Chair that makes him a Past Master, and not the degree ; while in the Chapter it is the degree, without any service whatever. The cases are not parallel : one has earned his position ; the other, has simply paid for a title. There is no reason, in Masonry or equity, why their privileges should be equal.

When the Grand Master is unable to attend to any duty requiring his presence at a distance from his home, he selects a proxy to act for him, and always, when possible to do so, the Master or Past Master of a Lodge. The same rule governs in the appointed officers of a Grand Lodge.

A Past Master is always eligible to reëlection without further service as Warden, either in the Lodge in which he originally served or in any other to which he may attach himself.

As a matter of courtesy, he is invited to a seat in the East, that he may aid the acting Master with his counsel, should it be needed in conducting the business of the Lodge.

Much argument has been had as to the right of a Past Master to a seat in his Grand Lodge, by virtue of his service in the Chair, and for some years the

Fraternity of New York were literally convulsed by the troubles arising from this source. The real question at issue, however, was not as to whether all Past Masters were entitled to life membership in the Grand Lodge, but whether those who had acquired that privilege under a law existing from the very foundation of the Grand Lodge, could be deprived of it by an enactment *ex post facto* in its nature and application. After long discussion, it was finally agreed, that while the Grand Lodge might amend its Constitution, so as to exclude all future Past Masters, it could not in equity take away rights which had been constitutionally acquired. With this agreement, the troubles in the Craft disappeared, as if by magic, and the Fraternity, again united, has ever since flourished as it never flourished before. There are still, we believe, one or two Grand Lodges where Past Masters are entitled to seats as such; but the general sense of the brethren appears now to be, that they have no privileges but those we have here enumerated.

THE WARDENS.

In every just and duly-constituted Lodge of Freemasons are two officers, styled respectively the Senior and Junior Warden. Second only in importance to the Master, a proper understanding and performance of their duties is essential to the welfare of the body.

Doctor OLIVER very happily terms them *Deputy Masters;* such in reality they are. During the business of the Lodge, and in what is technically termed *the work*, they are particularly called upon to assist in the preservation of order, and in the due performance of the ritual; and in case of the death, absence, or inability of the Master, they are authorized and required, in turn—that is, first the Senior Warden, and, in his absence, the Junior Warden—to succeed to all his powers and prerogatives, for the time being. We use the word *all* advisedly, because we have frequently heard it urged that the Warden, presiding in the absence of the Master, cannot confer degrees, partly because he has not received the degree of Past Master, and partly because the Regulations of 1721 provide that, in the absence of the Master, his power reverts to the last Past Master. We cannot write all that might be said in relation to the degree of Past Master, but it will answer our present purpose to say, that its reception is as much necessary to make a Master, as it is that he should have previously served a term as Warden, and that he should assent, in the presence of the brethren, to the questions put to him at his installation. Hence, though a brother should serve as Warden twenty years, and should all that time *act* as Master, he would not be Master *de facto*, nor at the close of that term be a Past Master, without

a regular election and installation as such, which
would include the degree in question. The degree,
then, is an absolute necessity to him who would be
Master, but not to a Warden temporarily called upon
to assume a contingency of his office.

The regulation referred to was evidently inserted
in the code by mistake, as it contains within itself a
flat contradiction of terms: for though it provides
that "the absent Master's authority reverts to the
last Master then present," yet it goes on to say, "he
cannot act until the said Senior Warden has once
congregated the Lodge, or, in his absence, the Junior
Warden." Dr. MACKEY remarks on this question:—

"The regulation is, however, contradictory in its provisions;
for if the 'last Master present' could not act—that is, could
not exercise the authority of the Master, until the Senior
Warden had congregated the Lodge—then it is evident that
the authority of the Master did not revert to him in an
unqualified sense; for that officer required no such concert or
consent on the part of the Warden, but could congregate
the Lodge himself.

"This evident contradiction in the language of the regulation probably caused, in a brief period, a further examination
of the ancient usage; and accordingly, on the 25th of No-
vember, 1723, a very little more than three years after, the
following regulation was adopted:

"'If a Master of a particular Lodge is deposed or dimits,
the Senior Warden shall forthwith fill the Master's chair till

the next time of choosing; and ever since, in the Master's absence, he fills the Chair, even though a former Master be present.' "*

But, admitting the Regulation of 1721 to be still in force, it is evident that the real power in the premises is vested in the Warden: for if he refuse to "congregate" the Lodge, then the Past Master would be powerless to do so, and would be without any Lodge to preside over. Such, except in England, is now the general sense of the Fraternity, and we therefore state, as the prerogatives of the Wardens:—

1. The right to assume the Chair in the absence of the Master, and to exercise, while so occupying it, all the powers that might of right be exercised by him, if personally present.

2. The right to represent the Lodge, in company with the Master, at all communications of the Grand Lodge. The same reasons apply here as in the case of the Master. They are a constituent part of the Grand Lodge, and it is their right, as well as duty, to be present at its communications. It is the practice in the Grand Lodge of New York, and we presume in those of other States, for either of the three (Master and Wardens) to cast the vote of his absent associates, on the principle that every Lodge is entitled to three votes.

* "Text-book of Masonic Jurisprudence."

3. The right, after regular installation and one year's service, to be elected Master in any regular Lodge with which they may affiliate, and which may choose to confer that honor upon them. And this, too, without regard to the period of time that may have elapsed between the close of the term of service as Warden and the election as Master.

4. In some Lodges, the Wardens are allowed to appoint the Deacons, but they are few in number, and the custom is likely to become altogether extinct.

According to the ritual, the Senior Warden is charged with the superintendence of the Craft while at labor, and particularly with the preservation of harmony by certain acts therein specified.

By the same authority, and in virtue of his installation charge, to the Junior Warden is committed the superintendence of the Craft during the hours of refreshment. From this has arisen the practice—for there is no written law on the subject—of requiring that all complaints against the brethren for infraction of our laws should be presented to the Lodge through him. This custom is now becoming general, and is every way to be commended; for if he is responsible for the proper conduct of the Craft while under his charge, when at refreshment or during the recess of the Lodge, it is but fair that he should present all complaints against them for infractions of the law committed during that time. It was the custom, within our experience, for the Junior Warden to perform the duty now assigned to the Senior Deacon, in the admission of visitors and the reception of candidates; and we recollect, too, that in some Lodges we have visited, the Wardens had truncheons, instead of columns. How the change has been brought about, we cannot say. In the French rite, the Wardens sit together in the West, and each has beside him one of the large columns, and, technically, the brethren on either side of the hall, under their superintendence, are said to be their columns.

In the absence of the Master, the Senior Warden succeeds to his place, but it does not follow that the Junior Warden thereby proceeds to occupy the Senior Warden's vacant station. The Junior Warden has certain well-defined duties, which, by his installation, he is bound to perform; among these is no provision for his occupancy of a higher station, save in the absence of both his superiors, when he proceeds to the East, and becomes acting Master. When, in the absence of the Master, the Senior Warden assumes the Chair, the prerogative of appointment vests in him, and he proceeds to fill his own vacant station by the appointment of a Senior Warden *pro tem.*

Finally, in the absence of the Master and Wardens,

6

it is now held that the Lodge cannot be opened, because there is no one authorized to congregate the brethren. We have already shown that, even if we admit the power of a Past Master to preside, he cannot do so until one of the Wardens has congregated the Lodge, and that is a power they cannot delegate.

The Wardens cannot resign; and in case of a vacancy in their offices, by death, suspension or expulsion, no election can be had to fill it, until the "regular time of choosing." They cannot resign, for the same reason that governs the Master, and, in fact, all the elected officers of the Lodge, because at their installation they have voluntarily promised to faithfully discharge the duties of their stations for the term of one year; to resign, would be to set this promise at naught, besides making the Lodge a party to the violation of a plighted word, and subjecting it to great inconvenience. Moreover, it is the prerogative of the Master to fill such vacancies by temporary appointments—it being understood, as a matter of course, that the brethren so appointed would exercise no powers, save that of assisting the Master during the meeting for which they might be appointed. In case of a session of the Grand Lodge, these appointees would not be representatives, but the Lodge would lose nothing thereby, for, as already said, the Master would cast the votes of the absent Wardens.

THE TREASURER.

In the thirteenth of the Regulations of 1721, it is
suggestively required that "the Treasurer should be
a man of good worldly substance;" and this, although
referring to the Treasurer of the Grand Lodge, would
seem to apply with equal force to the corresponding
officer in a subordinate one; for there is no trust
connected with the Lodge business which, as a general thing, is so well understood by the brethren as
its financial concerns. With greater tact, however,
than the ancients, we do not now so much regard
worldly substance as uprightness and sterling honesty
of character, which are considered better security
than mere wealth, especially as the Lodge, not being
recognized in law, there is no legal remedy against a
delinquent Treasurer. The Lodges in this country
give with a liberal hand, when a case of actual distress is brought to their knowledge; they take delight
in real jewels, and expensive furniture and clothing;
the consequence of which is, that the Treasurer is
rarely overburdened with such an amount of money
as to be likely, even if poor, to forfeit the reputation
of a life-time by yielding to the temptation of appro-
priating to his own use the contents of the Lodge
treasury. But even the comparatively small balance
which, as a general thing, stands to the Lodge credit,

is not left wholly to the keeping of the Treasurer, but, through the agency of Trustees, is placed in some public institution, where, in case of need, it may be called for, with a tolerable certainty that it will be forthcoming.

The office of Treasurer is of modern date, as may be seen from the fact, that so late as 1723, it was required that an Apprentice, at his making, should give something to be used for charitable purposes, which amount was to be taken in charge by the Master or Wardens, or the *Cashier*, if the members saw fit to appoint one,—the office being evidently of a temporary nature, and the Cashier to be appointed or not, as the brethren saw fit. Since that time, however, the importance of the office of Treasurer has so much increased, that he ranks immediately after the Wardens, and in English Lodges is the only officer, except the Master, required to be elected by ballot. His duties are fully set forth in the Installation Charge, and are entirely connected with the Lodge finances.

Under the general rule, that the elected officers cannot resign, no vacancy can occur in this office; but, in some jurisdictions, the Grand Lodge Regulations allow any officer, except the Master and Wardens, to vacate their offices by resignation. In such cases, the local statute will necessarily govern.

THE SECRETARY.

We regard the office of Secretary as, under our present organization, one of the most important in the Lodge. Like that of Treasurer, it can only be said to date from the revival of Masonry in 1717, the desultory manner in which Lodge meetings were held previous to that time requiring no minutes, and therefore no Secretary: in Article III. of the Old Regulations, to which we so frequently refer, there is, however, a provision for the appointment of some brother to keep, among other books, one in which shall be all the transactions proper to be written. This sufficiently describes the duty of the Secretary to show that, when Lodges assumed a regular organization under Warrants, his office became necessary to the preservation of the Lodge history and the prevention of confusion in its labors, and it is particularly on this ground that we consider him an important officer. The Lodge records are its current history, and, if well and neatly kept, ought to be a source of pride to the Lodge and of satisfaction to the Secretary, who should bear in mind that the lines he traces will live when the hand that made them is forgotten; that his children's children, grown to old men, may look upon his handiwork, and be grateful that, through it, the remembrance of the Lodge and

those who had guided its progress had been preserved. We have examined the minutes of some of
our old Lodges (still in existence), written more than
a century ago, the paper turned yellow and the
ink brown, but the language familiar as though
inscribed but yesterday, and it has seemed that
the very letters were links binding us with the past,
and proclaiming the abiding and imperishable nature
of our institution. It would, then, be well for every
Secretary of a Lodge to feel as if, in writing his
minutes, he were making history—carving, as it were,
with his pen, an unfading record of his Lodge and
himself. In the discharge of his duties, which are
purely clerical, he should exhibit order, neatness and
punctuality. By this, we mean that he should have
not only a place for every thing, but a regular system
of doing business; avoiding the slovenly fashion of
writing his minutes on odd scraps of paper, to be
found or not when needed, as the case may be; the
use of hieroglyphics that none but himself can read;
the bad habit of entering his minutes on the final
record, as the events occur, without waiting for the
confirmation of the Lodge, and thus incurring the
risk of erasures and interlineations, just as much out
of place there as they would be in a merchant's leger;
the trouble-breeding habit of trusting to memory—
which is always sure to desert him when its services

are most needed—particularly with reference to the collection of money. All the money of the Lodge necessarily passes through his hands: he should not only enter the amount received, in his cash-book, at the time, but he should also give his receipt for it, taking care also to exact a receipt from the Treasurer when he pays the funds over to him. It has been frequently urged in our presence that among Masons there should be no receipts exacted or given, which might be correct, if Masons were perfect; but as they are not exempt from the ordinary failings of humanity, it follows that the best-intentioned will sometimes make mistakes. Now, there is scarcely any mistake about which it is so difficult to convince a man as one in which the payment of money is involved. It is far from unfrequent for a member to insist that he has paid dues for a certain time, while the Secretary, finding no corresponding entry on his books, holds the opposite opinion with equal tenacity; ill feeling is often engendered, and a lurking suspicion soon finds a place in the hearts of the disputants; all of which may and should be prevented by the presentation of the Secretary's receipt, given at the time of payment.

It is customary, in the various foreign rites, to appoint an officer, known as the Keeper of Seals and Archives, who takes charge of all documents relating to the Lodge or its affairs, and who has also the Seal, which he alone is authorized to apply to all papers emanating from the Lodge or the Secretary. Among us, however, the Secretary has custody of the seal, and its application to the documents ordered by the Lodge is a prerogative of his office.

Finally, we find the duty of the Secretary correctly summed up in the maxim, "That it does not so much matter what the Lodge does, as what the Secretary records." He is to observe the will and pleasure of the Worshipful Master, and keep a just and true account of all things lawful to be written.

THE DEACONS.

There seems to be some question as to when the functions of the officers in Lodge, whom we style *Deacons*, were first made a part of our ritual. Dr. OLIVER appears to think their introduction as comparatively modern. One thing is certain, which is, that the part of the ritual assigned to the Senior Deacon is becoming greatly extended, and that, by apparently common consent, he now performs duties formerly devolving on the Junior Warden. The method of their appointment varies in different localities: in some, the Lodge elects; in others, the Master appoints; and, again, in others, the Master appoints the Senior, and the Senior Warden the Junior Deacon.

With their duties in the services of the ritual, we have nothing to do here; their remaining ones are principally to act,—the Senior Deacon as the proxy of the Master, by carrying messages for him about the Lodge, as desired; and the Junior Deacon, in a like capacity, for the Senior Warden. The Senior Deacon is placed at the right, and near the Master, that he may be ready to attend to his commands whenever issued. The Junior Deacon takes his position at the right of the Senior Warden, and is specially charged with the supervision of the outer door; it being his province to see that none pass or repass without the needful permission. The distinguishing feature of the Senior Deacon's office is, that it devolves upon him the reception of visiting brethren; and we here trespass on the good-nature of the reader to express a thought or two, which occur to us in this connection. Among the first things a brother does, on going to a strange place, is to ascertain the time and place of the Lodge meeting, and one of the pleasures he enjoys by anticipation is that of communing with the brethren in their Temple. Knowing this to be the case, it would naturally be supposed that the rites of hospitality would be administered with unusual grace; that the amenities of such occasions would be found attending the visiting brother, from the announcement of his name till he is prepared to go forth again to the outer world. In Europe, such is the case, and European Masons in this country are generally distinguished for the affability with which they receive and greet a visiting brother. But in American Lodges, the case is too often widely different, and the contrast does not place us in the most enviable light. When, among us, a visitor is announced, he is received, if a distinguished brother, with all the formal honors due to his position, but rarely anything farther; if merely a lay brother, he is, if known or vouched for, admitted, but is allowed to find accommodations as best he may; if the badge of labor be absent, he is very likely to be promptly admonished of that fact by the Master, as he will also be, if he omit any portion of the ceremonial observance depending on him, which is correct enough, but sometimes sadly embarrassing to a young Mason, to a timid one, or one who essays for the first time to put into practice the inculcations of the ritual. We need a little more politeness—a larger degree of that suavity which makes a bashful man feel at ease, and warms the heart of the stranger as though he were meeting with old friends. When a person calls upon us, at our house, we receive him in the best room, lead him to the best place in it, and make it our business to know that he is as comfortable as it is in our power to make him. When we go abroad, we expect similar attentions, and we mentally write that man down for a boor who is so far unacquainted with the customs of society as to neglect them. Now, the lodge-room is our Masonic home, and the politeness that we feel called upon to exercise in the domestic circle, ought to be equally manifest there. We should endeavor to make the visitor feel that we are glad to see him, glad to have him participate in the pleasant moments of our gathering, make him so enjoy his visit, that he will gladly seek an opportunity to renew it; that, at least, he will remember with pleasure his call at our assembly. All this can be done in the legitimate exercise of the functions of the Senior Deacon; and it is worth while for that officer to seek distinction, not only for his promptitude in obeying the orders of his superior, but also for the geniality of his reception of visiting brethren.

THE STEWARDS, or MASTERS OF CEREMONIES.

In the olden times, it was customary for Lodges to terminate their assemblies by a season of social enjoyment. In England, where the custom originated, it still prevails, and is commonly referred to as the "Knife-and-Fork degree." Less than half a century ago, the American Lodges considered their meetings incomplete without the table were spread in the anteroom, and the brethren furnished an opportunity to refresh themselves before departing for their homes. The wealthier Lodges had a regular commissariat, bought their stores at wholesale, and were always prepared to call from labor to refreshment, in the actual sense of the word; relics of which custom may still be met with in the shape of brightly-polished coffee-urns, inclosed in glass, and suspended on the *North* wall of the Lodge-room. Among a people who push things to such extremes as we do, conviviality must necessarily be abused, and that it was so, even when it flourished, we find from the songs published for use on those occasions, among which are several containing sneering allusions to those "who only go to Lodge to eat and drink." The practice, we are happy to say, has now fallen into disuse; the sentiment of the Craft is against it; and, that it may not be renewed, some at least of the Grand Lodges have forbidden by statute the introduction into the lodge-room or its precincts of any refreshment but water.

In those days, the Stewards were officers of great importance, being charged, as the name implies, with the duty of procuring the supplies and dispensing them to the brethren as occasion required. In addition to the principal duties of their office, they were also required to assist the other officers in the reception of visiting brethren, in the ceremonies pertaining to the several degrees, and in the dispensation of the Lodge charities.*   The office is still nominally retained in a majority of all the Lodges working in the so-called *York rite*, but in some jurisdictions the name of *Master of Ceremonies* is substituted, and it is probable that at no distant day that will become the accepted title of the officers in question.   With the change of name, there has been some change in the routine of their duties.   They do not now make any preparation for refreshments, nor do they have anything to do with the collection of dues, that being entirely in the hands of the Secretary, but in the reception of visitors and candidates, they are of great importance.   Our remarks on the attention to visitors, in the preceding section, will apply with equal force to these officers: their polite attentions and fraternal greetings on such occasions will rarely fail of appreciation by those to whom they are addressed; so, too, with candidates: if the duties of the Masters of Ceremonies are discharged in a courteous and

---

* In the WEBB installation service, (edition of 1816,) the duties of the Stewards are defined to be, "To assist in the collection of dues and subscriptions, to keep an account of the Lodge expenses, to see that the tables are properly furnished at refreshment, and that every brother is suitably provided for; and generally to assist the Deacons and other officers in performing their respective duties."   Nothing is said of Masters of Ceremonies, which fact sufficiently demonstrates that the change of name is one of extremely modern invention.

kindly manner, the effect to be thereby produced on
the mind of the novice will be correspondingly favorable; and, from this point of view, it is clearly the
duty of the Master, in the appointment of these
officers, to select brethren who by their manners are
capable of inducing a favorable opinion of the Lodge
in whose behalf they act, and of the Fraternity in
general.

THE TYLER.

This is one of the four indispensable officers of a
Lodge, and one whose functions and responsibilities
have undergone no change.*   He is generally, except
where the By-laws provide a different method, appointed by the Master, and, from the necessities of
his position, takes no part in the business of the
Lodge, and is not required to be a member of the
Lodge for which he acts.   The very first duty of the
brethren, when about to commence their labors, is to
be certain that the Tyler is at his post; for without
that certainty, no labor could be felt to be secure
from the interruptions of cowans and eavesdroppers.
He is the sentinel on the outposts, upon whose sleepless vigilance we depend for security.   But while he
is to be cautious and vigilant in preventing the ap-

* Except, perhaps, in the spelling of his title—Ti-ler—a mod-
ernism against which we respectfully protest.

proach of those who have not the necessary qualifications, he should also be courteous in his demeanor to all who may have occasion to address him. Politeness is not an expensive commodity, and every Tyler may, therefore, provide himself with an abundant supply, and find his profit in using it freely. The notion, which some Tylers we have met with seem to entertain, that it is a portion of their duty to imitate the fabled CERBERUS, is a fallacy that ought to be exploded. We have read of an executioner, who took off the heads of his victims with the most winning affability, and we know of no reason why a Tyler should be any more gruff than an executioner. Let him, if he will, imitate the conscript, who refused to allow the Emperor to pass without the countersign, but let him do it in a becoming manner, suffering none to pass without permission, but not acting as though he were bound to regard every one approaching him as desirous to pass his station at all hazards.

The Tyler is generally required, in addition to the duty of guarding the outer door, to serve all notices and summons, to take care of the jewels and implements against next preparation night, and in all things to be guided by the will and pleasure of the Worshipful Master.

OTHER OFFICERS.

The officers above enumerated are all that, strictly speaking, can be said to be required in a Masonic Lodge, or to have any real official *status* in it; but while these are necessary to make a perfect Lodge, it is left to the discretion of the brethren to name others, which is, in most cases, done to give a *quasi* official station to some brother or brethren whom the Lodge desire in that way to honor. Thus, when a minister of the Gospel is initiated in or affiliates with a Lodge, it is not uncommon for the Master to appoint him *Chaplain*, and place in his charge the religious ceremonies of the society. There is a propriety in this that commends the practice. The prayers and invocations of the ritual are more solemn and effective when pronounced by one who is known to have received holy orders. We may even go further, and say that, when it is possible to secure the services of such a brother, it ought always to be done; it being understood that if he really love Masonry, he will, in the discharge of his duties, exemplify only "that Religion in which all men agree," leaving the particular opinions of the brethren to themselves.

For similar reasons, we have known a brother to be appointed *Physician* to his Lodge. We could never imagine any Masonic reason for the creation of such an office, except, perhaps, that his professional talents might be called into operation in the examination of the physical qualifications of candidates.

Some Lodges appoint a *Marshal*, who is to take charge of all processions and public ceremonials of the Lodge. If these occasions were of frequent occurrence—as, happily, they are not—it might be well to have an officer who would make himself competent to officiate; but as it is, when Lodges do appear in public—as at a funeral, for instance—a temporary appointment seems to answer all the requirements.

The Board of Trustees, though not really officers, but rather a kind of standing committee, occupy most important relations to the Lodge, particularly when, by a long and successful career, its funds and properties have accumulated to a considerable amount. Lodges, under our civil law, not being incorporated, are not recognized as having a legal *status*, or the rights that ensue : hence, they cannot acquire or dispose of real estate, or invest their funds, except through the agency of Trustees. It is, therefore, of moment that not only should such a Board exist, but that it should be composed of prudent and discreet brethren, who will appreciate the confidential nature of the trust reposed in them, and be governed not only by a high sense of honor, but by a desire to forward the best interests of their Lodge. The first and strongest claim upon the capital of a Masonic Lodge is that of a worthy brother in distress, or that of his widow or orphans in destitute circumstances. Money for such a purpose loses its ordinary character, and becomes a trust, sacred as the fires of Vesta, and he who wrongfully appropriates or carelessly administers it, acquires, at the same time, the contempt of every right-minded Mason.

It is usual for the Lodge property to be placed in the custody of the Trustees, and they also receive and invest, as the Lodge may direct, all its surplus funds.

The manner of their appointment and their tenure of office depend altogether upon the By-laws of the Lodge.

SECTION II. — ELECTIONS.

Of the officers named in the preceding section, the Master, Wardens, Treasurer, and Secretary are, as a general rule, required to be elected by ballot. The others are elected or appointed, as the Constitution of the Grand Lodge may permit or the By-laws direct. In England, only the Master and Treasurer are elected by ballot, the remaining officers, except the Tyler, being appointed by the Master.

The elections are required to be held annually, at

such time as may be prescribed by the Regulations of the Grand Lodge; generally at the stated communication next preceding the festival of St. JOHN the Evangelist (27th of December), though in some cases on the day of the festival itself, and the installation must either take place at once, or within some reasonable period thereafter. Until such installation takes place, it is a settled rule that the old officers hold over, the installation being the completion of the election, and the contract—so to speak—on the part of the officer not only to accept the election, but faithfully to discharge the duties of his office for the term of one year, or until his successor has fulfilled the like conditions; for which reason, as we have already stated, an installed officer cannot and ought not to resign. It is doubtful whether there is any law for this, older than the present century, but it is a regulation universally sanctioned in the United States, and it has, therefore, all the force of a Landmark.

Should a Subordinate Lodge, from any cause, fail to comply with the Grand Lodge Regulations, as to the time of election, it has no authority within itself to correct the default, but must apply to the Grand Master or his Deputy for a Dispensation to authorize an election at a time other than that specified in the Constitution.

At every election, each member of the Lodge in good standing is entitled to one vote. On this point, two questions have been extensively argued :—1st, Who is the judge, and what is good standing, so far as it is applicable to voting at an election for officers? and, 2d, Are blank ballots, cast at such an election, votes? These questions are of sufficient importance to warrant their examination in this place.

It is held, by one side, that a member is in good standing for all purposes, so long as his name remains upon the roll, or so long as he has not, after due trial, been suspended or expelled for unmasonic conduct : and by the other—with which we agree—that a Lodge has a right to inflict a lesser penalty than suspension for a delinquency that may be provided for in its By-laws. It is admitted that a Lodge has a right to require the payment of an annual sum (called dues) by each of its members, the amount of which, and the manner of its payment, is of necessity left to the Lodge. In Lodges where such dues are exacted,* it is now the common practice to insert a clause in the By-laws, depriving those in arrears for a specified period of their votes at elections for officers, until such arrearages have been paid. Now, we cannot understand why, if a Lodge has the right to enact a

* In Rhode Island, and, we think, Connecticut, the members of Lodges are not required to pay dues.

By-law requiring the payment of dues, it should not also have the right to punish, by a reasonable penalty, a neglect or refusal to comply with the law. Every Master Mason is informed at his raising that, after signing the By-laws, he will be considered a member in good standing, entitled to all the rights and privileges of the Lodge, and subject to all its rules and regulations. The Lodge here evidently reserves the right to judge of his good standing in the future by putting him in mind of his obligation to "stand to and abide by" the rules and regulations. He signs the official copy of the By-laws, in token of his assent to their provisions, and of his intention to maintain them; he is furnished with a copy, (and if he does not read it, the fault is his,) and thus he is fairly held to know them, (just as, in the State, every citizen is assumed to know the law, and cannot plead ignorance of it as a justification of its infraction,) and to accept of certain privileges—among which is the right to vote—on condition of the performance of certain acts by him. It is, therefore, submitted that, in all fairness, a member who fails or neglects to pay his dues as required by the By-laws, violates a promise voluntarily given by him, and has no right to complain of the enforcement of a penalty, which he had likewise agreed to in advance, and the disability accruing from which can be removed at once by the payment of a sum justly due. It will be understood, as a matter of course, that where the non-payment arises from positive inability, it would not come within the terms of the regulation, because it would then be neither refusal nor neglect. The right to vote for the officers of a Lodge is evidently a household matter, and, strictly speaking, concerns only the members of the particular Lodge: it is but just, therefore, that they should control a subject in which they alone are directly interested.

The ballot for candidates is widely different: in that case, it is a landmark that every brother present should give his consent, and no By-law can change a fundamental law; but the rules governing the election of officers, being of modern date, are subject to no such restriction. For these reasons, we are of opinion that the Lodge is the judge of the qualification of its own voters, and that a brother who has willfully neglected or refused to comply with the By-law which requires the payment of arrearages as a qualification to vote at an election for officers, is not a qualified voter, and, to that extent, not in good standing.

Secondly. Are blank ballots, cast at an election for officers, votes? We think they are, and our reasons are few, and easily comprehended. Let us first explain that, by a ballot, we understand a slip of paper,

when the election is for officers; when it is for candidates, we use the same word to signify white and
black balls, used for the purpose of voting. A ballot
represents a brother's vote, which is the expression
of whatever opinion he may entertain, and which he
has a right to express without let or hindrance.
Every qualified voter is entitled to one vote, and the
successful candidate must have a majority of all the
votes cast. Now, suppose an election about to take
place, the first thing is to ascertain the number of
voters, suppose we say twenty, of which eleven would
of course be necessary to the success of any candidate. The roll is called, and every brother having
deposited his ballot, the tellers announce twenty
votes; they proceed to canvass, and find that John
Smith has ten votes, William Brown nine, and that
there is one blank. Under these circumstances, there
could be no election; for no one could be said to
have received a majority of all the votes cast, nor
could the brother who deposited the blank ballot be
lawfully deprived of his franchise: he had a right to
vote as he pleased, and because there was no name
on the slip of paper used by him, it was none the
less his vote, and had been formally deposited by him
as such. Suppose that, instead of an absolute blank,
he had written the name of Mary Smith upon it;
there would then be no question as to its being a

vote; yet Mary Smith could not, by any possibility, be a candidate, and a vote for such a personage would be just as much a vote thrown away, as a blank would be. Take another view: Suppose Smith to have received eleven votes, and blank nine. Could it be pretended that Smith would be unanimously elected? Certainly not; for there would be nine voters, who, although they did not choose to vote for any one else, clearly did not vote for him, and yet the expression of their opinion could not be ignored. The true rule is, to ascertain the whole number of votes cast, and then require the successful candidate to have received a majority of that number, whether the minority be blanks or otherwise. When, on a question pending, the vote is taken by ballot, blank ballots are always counted as in the affirmative.

It is held that, as nominations for office are permitted in the Grand Lodge, by analogy, it is proper to nominate in the subordinate. As there is no law against such a practice, there is nothing to prevent it but the good sense of the brethren, which, so far as our experience goes, has prevailed, though we know there are jurisdictions where the practice of nominations is common. To our mind, the idea of making open nominations for the officers, at an election in a particular Lodge, is utterly repugnant—at complete variance with that calm dignity which ought to characterize all the proceedings. It reduces us at once to the level of the ordinary associations of men, and divests us of an attribute to which we ought to cling with immovable tenacity. Moreover, it is a practice for which necessity cannot be urged. The custom of calling off for a few moments, previous to depositing the ballots, affords an opportunity for consultation, and then, labor being resumed, the silent ballot is more in accordance with the spirit of the Craft than a resort to the practices of the outside world could be. We have been present at a great many elections in Subordinate Lodges, but never yet at one where open nominations were made, and it appears to us that such an act would shock our idea of the proprieties of such occasions. We earnestly hope that no Lodge will commence the practice, and that those that have been accustomed to it will see the propriety of its speedy abandonment.

Much has been written to prove that a brother elected or appointed to office is bound to serve. It is sufficient to say, that there is no law for such assertion, but that every Mason is free to accept office or not. When, however, a brother has been chosen to aid in the labors of the Lodge, in any station for which his capacities fit him, he ought, if possible, to accept, and thus prove that he has its welfare at heart.

7

The results of an election should be immediately communicated by the Secretary to the Grand Secretary, under his official seal.

Elections are always to be held in a Lodge opened on the third degree.

In some Lodges, the Treasurer and Secretary are required to receive and canvass the ballots; but it is a better rule to appoint tellers from among the brethren, leaving the officers to occupy their respective stations.

SECTION III.—INSTALLATION.

The ceremony of installation, which, as we have already remarked, is the completion of the election, is, therefore, indispensable to the officers elect; for without it they cannot legally enter upon the duties of their respective offices. For this reason, it should be performed at the earliest convenient time after the completion of the balloting.

The act of installation, as will be seen by reference to the *Manual*, consists of the presentation of the officers elect to the installing officer, on whose demand the brethren acknowledge that they are the persons elected, and that they (the brethren) remain satisfied with their choice. (This is the proper time to make objections, if any are to be made, against any irregularity that may have occurred on the balloting; for it is held that if the installation be allowed to proceed without objection, it will then be too late to make complaint.) In a covenant by the officers elect, faithfully to discharge the duties of the several trusts for the term of their election. In the public acknowledgment by the Master elect of his acceptance of and submission to the Charges and Regulations, as Masters have done in all ages before him. In an appropriate Charge to the Master and each of the officers. And, finally, in rendering homage and due respect to the new officers.

All these ceremonies, except the qualification of the officers, may be performed in public; and we speak from much experience when we say, that the effect of such a course, where properly conducted, is always beneficial—as tending to convince the world that the duties and responsibilities exacted of our officers are of a nature to be commended; that we seek to maintain no greater secrecy as to our proceedings than is necessary to preserve the institution from innovation; and, as having a tendency, by requiring the officers to assume their trusts in the presence of their families and friends, to impress with greater force upon their minds the serious nature of their undertaking. Public intallations may be enlivened with appropriate music, and should be accompanied by an address, in which the nature and design of **Freemasonry and** other kindred subjects may be treated.

It is the province of the retiring **Master** to install his successor, but he may, **if he** please, delegate this power to any **Past Master,** but not to any brother of inferior **rank ;** or, if desired, the new Master, after his own installation, may install the other officers.

There are some who hold that, in case of reëlection, no installation is needed; but when we reflect that the election and the covenant are for a specified term, we must admit that, with the close of the term, the obligation ends, and that, therefore, a **new election,** beginning as it does a new term, requires a **new covenant and a** corresponding installation; nor **do** we appreciate the assertion that a man cannot be his own successor; for he commences the new term just **as any** other person would, or just as if he had never occupied the station **before. We** apprehend that **where a** President of the United States or the Governor of a **State** is reëlected, he is required to again assume the oath of office, as though he **had never** been inaugurated before, and the **cases are** exactly parallel.

There are some jurisdictions where installation is allowed to be assumed by proxy. The majority of Grand Lodges are, however, averse to such proceeding; and we do not see how a man can take upon himself an obligation by the lips of another, or how he could be legally held for the infraction of a vow he had not personally pronounced.

Immediately after the installation, the retiring officers transfer to their successors all the books, money, and property of the Lodge that may have been in their possession.

CHAPTER V.

Lodge Meetings.

THE assemblies of a Lodge, technically termed COMMUNICATIONS, are of two kinds—*called* and *stated*.

Called meetings, or meetings of emergency, are entirely within the discretion of the Master, or of the Warden acting in his absence, as to time, but they are required to be held at the place usually occupied by the Lodge. As a general rule, no business can be transacted at such meetings, except that stated in the summons or call; but there are some things that cannot be done there, even if mentioned in the summons: as, the presentation of petitions for initiation or adjoining; the appointment of committees to act on such petitions; the ballot on report of committees of investigation, previously appointed at a stated communication; the dispensation of charity, or any other disposal of the Lodge funds. This last item, and perhaps some others, may be considered in a called Lodge, but they can only be finally and lawfully acted upon at a stated communication. In like manner, the minutes may be read and corrected, if necessary, but they can only be confirmed at a following regular assembly. The legitimate action of a called meeting may, therefore, be said to be limited to, the conferring of degrees on candidates previously regularly elected, the giving instruction in the work and lectures, and the public ceremonials of the Craft, as Dedications, Installations, and the burial of the dead.

Stated meetings are the regular assemblies of the Lodge at the time and place named in the Warrant, and more particularly specified in the By-laws. They should occur at least once in each calendar month, and not more than twice in the same period of time. We are aware that some of the finest and most flourishing Lodges hold weekly communications; but we think that, all things considered, it will be found wisest not to make too frequent calls upon the time and attention of the members, lest, in the end, they weary of a pleasure too frequently enjoyed, and little by little lose their interest in the Lodge and in the institution. It is difficult to maintain the interest in weekly meetings, except by a constant succession of "work," which is wearisome to the officers and dangerous to the Lodge; for there is less likelihood of careful examination into the qualifications of candidates, and of due proficiency before advancement, where the staple attraction is the conferring of degrees, for which other and more important matters must, almost of necessity, be sacrificed. Let us not be misunderstood: we do not assert that such is always the case, but that it is so, sometimes, we know; that it may be so frequently, there is danger. One evil alone that grows out of weekly meetings, more than counterbalances all the good to be expected of them, and that is, the reception of a petition at one meeting, and the report of committee, ballot for, and initiation of a candidate at the next; or with the lapse of only seven days between the petition of a candidate and his actual initiation into the Fraternity. We know that this is done in New York, and it is within the letter of the Constitution, but it is so near making Masons at sight, that the difference is hardly worth mentioning. Anything less than a month between the petition and the ballot is a violation of the Old Regulations; and although Grand Lodge Constitutions may permit an abbreviation of that time, Lodges should, for their own safety and stability, waive the privilege, and act upon the old law. They will be the better enabled to do this, by having their stated meetings less frequently than once a week. Finally, if it is thought indispensable to hold weekly meetings, let the first one in each month be the stated communication, devoted to the legislative business of the Lodge, and the others, special meetings for the conferring of degrees and exemplification of the work and lectures; both the business and work would thus stand a chance of being well done, and the value of the maxim, that "Masonry is never in a hurry," be made manifest.

The first business at all meetings, after the congregation of the Lodge, is, of course, the formula of opening, which we take occasion to say should never be performed in a slovenly manner, nor hastily slurred over, but given in ample detail, for the benefit of the uninstructed brethren, and for the credit of the Lodge and its officers. The introduction of music in this, as well as in other appropriate portions of the ceremonies, is, in our judgment, to be highly commended. When well performed, either by the united voices of the brethren, or with the accompaniment of an organ or harmonium, it seems to predispose the mind to the exercise of those qualities that ought especially to distinguish the assemblies of the Craft. There are those who object to it, because it is made the means of introducing some inelegant doggerel, but we are inclined to regard the sentiment, rather than the versification of what we sing: if the idea sought to be inculcated is correct, and the music good, the rhyme is of small consequence.

There is a practice in many Lodges of calling the roll of officers immediately after the Lodge is declared open, which, although it has no legal sanction, is nevertheless not without its use as an inducement to those brethren to be promptly at their stations, that they may answer when called, and by their example lead the members generally to be punctual in their attendance.

The business of the meeting always commences by the reading of the minutes of the last stated communication, and of those of any special meeting that may have intervened, that the latter may be approved, and that the Lodge may be governed by the former as to any unfinished business requiring its attention, as reports of standing or special committees, or any other item of Lodge business. In this respect, the qualities of a good Secretary will at once be manifested by the orderly arrangement of the various topics that may have been acted upon at the previous communication. Some Secretaries write their entire minutes in one paragraph, as if the economy of half a sheet of paper that might be consumed in properly displaying them would materially affect the Lodge revenues. Properly, each item should form a separate paragraph, and when one is finished, a blank line should be left before commencing another. A wide margin is also to be recommended, that brief notes may be written opposite the important paragraphs, to indicate their tenor. The object of these marginal notes is, to enable the Secretary or others to discover the record of any particular circumstance without being obliged to read through the whole body of the minutes. Brevity—that is, so much as is consistent with clearness—ought to be the aim of the brother who writes the minutes; neatness and system in their arrangement always attract commendation. At the bottom of the last page of the minutes of each communication should be entered, in full, the names of all brethren who have paid money to the Secretary, and opposite to their names the amount so paid, as also the items of disbursement ordered by the Lodge. These items, when so entered, are convenient for reference; and after having been read to and approved by the Lodge, are vouchers of the Secretary's correctness. Finally, the Master is to observe that the record is correct, both as to what is written and what is omitted, before he allows it to be confirmed.

After the reading of the minutes, the proper opportunity is afforded for the admission of visitors, as it can then be done with less interruption to the proceedings, than when the Lodge has entered upon the transaction of its regular business. No alarm should be attended to during the ceremony of opening or closing; during the reading of the minutes; while a brother is addressing the Lodge, or while the Master is engaged in conferring degrees; nor should any countenance be given to the practice of entering or

retiring from the Lodge during the most solemn part
of the ceremonies. A proper respect for the Master
and the proprieties of such occasions ought in themselves to be a sufficient restraint ; but when they fail,
the authority of the Master should at once be inter-
posed. Visitors may, of course, be admitted at any
time, if the Master choose to allow it ; but it is better
for all concerned that brethren should be at the hall
at the time appointed for the opening, in order that
they may be examined, if necessary, and admitted at
an early period of the communication.

Behavior, in the Lodge and out of it, is so fully
treated in the sixth of the Ancient Charges, that we
need do no more in this place than refer to that
authority.

The method of voting depends upon the subject
on which the vote is to be taken : thus, in elections
of candidates and officers, ballots are used, which, in
one case, are slips of paper, on which the voter writes
his preference, or which he leaves blank; in the other,
white and black balls, the white being used to signify
the affirmative, or consent ; the black, the negative,
or rejection. On all other questions, the vote is usually taken by uplifted hands, which, if required, the
Deacons count. Much argument has been wasted in
the attempt to demonstrate the proper hand to be
uplifted—some inclining to the right ; others, with

equal plausibility, to the left. We have never been able to perceive that it makes any difference which hand is used.

Much of the Lodge business is performed, in its details, by reference to committees. Committees are of two kinds—standing and special. Standing committees are usually appointed on election night, and serve for the official year—the purpose of their appointment being indicated by the By-laws. Special committees are named as occasion may require, and are generally discharged when the particular item of business placed in their charge is disposed of. All committees are appointed by the Master, unless he waive the right. It is the custom for the brother first named in the appointment of a committee to act as Chairman. Reports of committees should always be reduced to writing, not only to avoid any misunderstanding as to their sentiments, but for the convenience of the Secretary and that of the brethren. All members of committees are in honor bound to the faithful discharge of the trust imposed on them, and should make their report with all proper exactitude and dispatch.

In the discussions that sometimes arise in a Lodge it is, as we have already shown, the prerogative of the Master to mark the limits of debate, and keep the brethren within them. Few men, however, are gifted with the powers of discrimination necessary to the exercise of so difficult a supervision, and, therefore, some rules are sought for which shall suffice to keep the debate within due bounds, and their observance be at once a restraint on the brethren and an assistance to the presiding officer. The mind thus naturally reverts to what is termed "Parliamentary law," and the question arises, "How far may it safely be used in the business of a Masonic Lodge?" This question has been most ably and satisfactorily answered by M. W. Bro. BENJAMIN B. FRENCH, in an article published in the *American Quarterly Review of Freemasonry*. We feel that we are doing the Craft a service by transferring to these pages its most important suggestions.

"No body of men," (says Bro. FRENCH,) "no matter how small, or how well disposed to be orderly it may be, can be kept in order for the transaction of business, and the debate which necessarily accompanies it, without a presiding officer; and no presiding officer, be his talent and capacity for presiding what they may, can keep order unless he be governed by fixed rules and principles, admitted to be binding by those over whom he presides. Therefore, we find the custom to be universal, after the organization of any assembly of individuals, of adopting rules for government, by which they impose a duty on their presiding officer of administering, and on themselves of obeying, the rules thus made. In ordinary public bodies, these rules are temporary, lasting only during the legal existence of the body which they are formed to govern. The House of Representatives of the United States becomes a new legislative body every two years, and is only governed by the general parliamentary law until either the rules of the preceding House are adopted, or a new code formed. The Senate, being a permanent body, is always governed by the same rules until it sees fit to alter or renew them.

" Masonic bodies are somewhat like the Senate, in this latter particular. When once formed, they remain Lodges, Chapters, etc., forever. Therefore, the rules and regulations by which they are to be governed, ought to be permanent and uniform. I have noticed, within a few years, a new feature adopted by some of the governing Masonic bodies, in the formation of 'model by-laws,' on which the Subordinates are to found their codes. This is an excellent plan, inasmuch as it tends to create a uniformity of government in the jurisdictions wherein it operates. But by-laws are one thing, and rules of government, while the body is assembled for business, another.

" My design in this paper is to present my own views in relation to the application of regular parliamentary law, so far as it will apply to the government of Masonic bodies.

" The term Parliamentary Law originated by being the designation of the peculiar law which governed and governs the proceedings of the British Parliament. Laws and rules adopted by that body became by degrees the governing law of all deliberative assemblies, so far as they would apply:

and as soon as our forefathers so far established governments
on this side of the Atlantic as to need rules and regulations,
they adopted those of the mother-country; and thus the law
of parliament became, in a measure, the governing law of
American deliberative assemblies; and the law of parliament
has come to be a general term, applicable to all well-established rules and regulations adopted by legislatures.

"'The *dictum* of HATSELL—the best English authority on
precedents extant—that 'it is much more material that there
should be a rule to go by, than what that rule is,' is a sound
principle, and applies as well to the government of a Masonic
Lodge as to the House of Commons of Great Britain.

" All regular meetings of Masonic bodies are fixed by their
by-laws, and the records of the body should always show,
either that the meeting was held, or the reason why it was
not. It is well known to every well-informed Freemason,
that a certain number must be present before a Lodge can
be opened, and that it requires also the presence of certain
officers: therefore, no parliamentary rule applies to the con-
vening of a Lodge. The rule, that a faithful record shall be
kept of what is proper to be written, is a Masonic one; and
the period of no regular meeting should be suffered to pass,
even though the Lodge be not opened, without a statement,
as full as may be, on the record-book, giving the facts as they
occurred, that when the proper inspecting officer makes his
annual visit, he may see as well what has been omitted to be
done that ought to have been done, and the reasons therefor,
as what has actually been done.

" The Lodge having been duly opened, it becomes at once

a de.iberative assembly for any business that may legitimately come before it. The Master is the presiding officer, and the floor is open, under the restrictions of the by-laws, to any member who may desire to submit any proposition proper for consideration. And here the parliamentary rules apply in all their force.

"I will here quote those rules, substituting the words 'Master' and 'Brother' for *Speaker* and *Member*.

"When the Master is seated in his chair, every brother is to sit in his place.

"When any brother means to speak, he is to stand up in his place, and address himself, not to the Lodge, or any particular brother, but to the Master, who calls him by his name, that the Lodge may take notice of who it is that speaks.

"When a brother stands up to speak, no question is to be put; but he is to be heard.

"[This rule closes with the words, 'unless the House over-rule him.' It is not customary or proper for the Lodge to overrule any brother in debate. If the Master deem the debate irrelevant, he has full power to call the brother to order, and to keep him within the bounds of order, or to silence him in a manner known only to Masons. From the Master's decision there is no appeal to the Lodge.] *

"If two or more brethren rise to speak nearly together, the Master determines who was first up, and calls him by name; whereupon he proceeds, unless he voluntarily sits down, and gives way to the other.

"[Here again the House can overrule the Speaker, and

decide which member was first up. But the Lodge cannot
overrule the Master.]

"By the parliamentary law, no one may speak more than
once, to the same question, on the same day. This is a very
wholesome provision, and, unless there be some particular
provision in the by-laws touching this point, it would be well
for the Master, when he thinks precious time is being wasted
in debate, to enforce it. This is a matter, however, that I
consider altogether discretionary with the Master, and in
which he should always be governed by the peculiar circumstances of the time. Explanation, as to what has been said,
is always permitted.

"If the Master rises to speak, the brother standing up
must sit down, that he may be first heard.

"No one is to speak impertinently or beside the question,
superfluously or tediously.

"No one is to disturb another in his speech by hissing,
coughing, spitting, or whispering to another, nor to stand up
or interrupt him; nor to pass between the Master and the
speaking brother, nor to go across the Lodge-room, nor to
walk up and down it.

"If a brother, in debate, use any improper language, any
brother may call him to order, if the Master do not; and if
there is any dispute as to the language used, it would be
well to have the language-taken down by the brother calling
to order, that the Master may consider it carefully before
coming to a decision.

"As the rules of Freemasonry allow no appeal from the
Master to the Lodge, it behooves every Master to make his

decisions with great care, and after full consideration; and, although no appeal can be taken, the Master may, before his decision, ask experienced members of the Lodge to aid him with their opinions, and they are bound to respond. The Master may, if he see fit, express an opinion to the Lodge, and ask its advice, prior to making his decision.

"Any brother may present a petition to the Lodge, if properly signed and vouched, at the time when petitions are in order, or he may hand it to the Secretary, and have it presented through him. After it is received, it is for the Lodge to determine what is to be done with it. If no question is made by any brother, the petition is referred to the Master as a matter of course; and when reported upon, the report is open to amendment and debate, and to final action by the body to which it is made.

"Upon the presentation of a petition, any brother may raise the question, and, in that case, the Master is bound to put the question: 'Shall the petition be received?' If not received, no further action can be had relative to it, and it remains in the hands of the one who presented it, to be disposed of as he thinks proper."

*   *   *   *   *   *   *   *   *

"'Committees of the Whole' are out of place in a Masonic body. Lodges can only do business with the *Master* in the chair; for, let who will preside, he is, while occupying the chair, *Master*—invested with supreme command, and emphatically 'governs the Lodge.' Any committee presupposes a 'Chairman,' and no Freemason would feel at home, were he presided over by a 'Chairman.'"

"There is a difference between *accepting* and *adopting* a report. If nothing is said, it is considered as *accepted* as soon as made. If it closes with resolutions, and the report itself requires no definite legislation, the question is on agreeing to the resolutions. If the report itself embodies legislation, and there are also resolutions attached, the question is on *adopting* the report, and agreeing to the resolutions. If no resolutions are attached, and the report recommends no action, its *acceptance*, either tacitly or by a vote, disposes of it. If it requires action, then a vote must be taken on its adoption, to make it binding. If it is upon a petition for admission, no matter whether favorable or unfavorable, the question is on proceeding to ballot for the candidate, unless a motion is made to dispose of the report in some other manner.* Reports may be recommitted at any time before the final action upon them."   *   *   *   *   *

"Motions, in a Masonic body, are governed by precisely the same rules as in a parliamentary body. Any member of the body can make a motion, and it must be seconded by another member, (the presiding officer can second it, if he pleases,) before it is in possession of the body. If in order, of which the presiding officer must be the judge, it is then debatable, or may be put to the question, if no debate is offered. If the presiding officer require it, all motions must be put in writing before being acted upon.

Resolutions and Orders are governed by precisely the

---

* We can imagine no other disposition of such a report, except to lie upon the table temporarily, or to recommit for further examination. Its final disposition must be by ballot, for the petition on which it is based cannot be withdrawn.

same rules as motions; they are often only motions reduced to writing: for instance, a brother may move that the Lodge proceed to ballot for a candidate, or he may introduce a resolution in writing to do the same thing. Resolutions generally express opinions, and motions may apply to resolutions, as 'a motion to amend,' 'to lie upon the table,' 'to postpone,' etc., but resolutions cannot apply to motions.

"Orders are only used when the body commands, as, '*Ordered*,' that the Secretary do so and so, etc.

"Freemasonry knows no 'previous question,' and no Masonic body should ever tolerate it."   *   *   *

"The Masonic rule should be, that where well-settled parliamentary principles can be properly applied to the action of Masonic bodies, they should always govern; but they should never be introduced where they, in any way, interfere with the established customs or landmarks of Masonry, or with the high prerogatives of the Master."

To the above we subjoin, for the sake of completeness, the following, by Dr. MACKEY:

When a motion has once been made, and carried in the affirmative or negative, it is in order for any member who voted in the majority to move for a reconsideration thereof at the same communication.

When an amendment is proposed, a member who has already spoken to the main question may again speak to the amendment.

When a blank is to be filled, and various propositions have been made, the question must be taken first on the highest sum or the latest time proposed.

Any member may call for a division of the question, which division will take place, if a majority of the members consent.

A motion to lie on the table is not debatable.

A motion to adjourn is unmasonic, and cannot be entertained.

The business of the meeting is concluded by the reading of the minutes, in order that any errors or omissions may be corrected, while the brethren are present who have taken part in the proceedings. They are then approved, which being done, we hold that they cannot subsequently be altered, even though a mistake of omission or commission should be made manifest. The reason is, that the minutes of a Lodge are the legal record of its transactions, and on Masonic trials are admitted as evidence: if they were subject to alteration at will, they could have no such value, because there would then be no certainty that the minutes produced were in the same condition that they were at the time they were recorded. Where a palpable error is ascertained, it can be noted in the minutes of the next communication, and when approved by the Lodge, will stand as the legal correction of the former minutes.

Finally, the ceremony of closing is to be observed with the same care as that of opening, and, as before hinted, it should be the endeavor of Master and brethren to have it always take place at a reasonably early hour.

CHAPTER VI.

The Floor Members.

WE have, in a previous chapter, stated our belief in the doctrine that, as in the State, the original sovereignty resides in the people, so in Masonry, it belongs to the members of the subordinate or particular Lodges, but the extent to which it may be exercised by its original custodians, is now a very different matter from what it was previous to the revival of 1717. At that period, Lodges being merely temporary gatherings for the one purpose of conferring the E. A. degree, membership and its consequences, as now understood, were unknown. Each individual acted for himself, and entirely without control or restraint, nor were there any but the most general relations between individual Masons, except when a number gave their consent to the initiation of a profane, and attended a meeting held under the authority of the civil magistrates, to witness and assist in the performance of that ceremony.* The

---

* The four old Lodges, which are so often referred to in connection with the formation of the Grand Lodge of England, would seem to have been an exception, so far as permanent organization

great body of the Craft was then composed of Apprentices, or Masons of the first degree, and the Annual Assembly was a gathering of the whole Fraternity, or so many of them as chose to attend. As there were no permanent Lodges, each brother represented his own interest at the General Assembly, and the legislation must necessarily have been of the most primitive character. When, however, the Grand Lodge was established, and Lodges became permanent organizations, under authority of Warrants issuing from the supreme body, the general powers which had previously been exercised by individuals, were merged in the Lodges, and their powers were in turn circumscribed by delegation of a portion of their rights to the superior authority of the Grand Lodge, so that the individual sovereignty may now, in general terms, be said to be only exercised in regard to candidates for initiation or adjoining, in the selection of officers, and in instructing them for their government in Grand Lodge. In those days, too, the Grand Lodge reserved the right to confer the degrees of Fellow Craft and Master Mason, the applications for which, as the Fraternity increased in numbers and

is concerned. Their origin and transactions are, however, involved in a great deal of mystery, which it is not in our power to clear up. We are not writing history, and, therefore, only speak in a general sense.

new Lodges were formed, becoming too numerous for its capacity, it was obliged to relieve itself of the burden, by empowering the Lodges to confer the whole three degrees, and confining itself to the functions now exercised by Grand Lodges.

The result of this change has been, that in all Lodges deriving their existence from the English system, as ours do, Master Masons have taken the place formerly occupied by Apprentices, though in jurisdictions where the Scottish or Ancient and Accepted Rite prevails, the change is not so manifest; Apprentices in those jurisdictions still participating in all the business of the Lodge, except conferring the two superior degrees, and even holding office.

Lodges are, therefore, now composed of Entered Apprentices, Fellow Crafts and Master Masons, and the latter may be divided into two classes—affiliated and non-affiliated. The officers are chosen from the affiliated Master Masons, because they alone are in reality members of the Lodge; but, as we have already spoken of the officers, we shall be understood as in this chapter referring particularly to what are termed "floor members:" that is, Masons not holding any office, or, in military parlance, "the rank and file."

As there are peculiarities attached to each class, we shall give each a separate consideration.

8

SECTION I.—ENTERED APPRENTICES.

The name applied to the brother who has received the first degree **of Masonry**, appears to signify that he is one who has entered the Fraternity, but only in the character of a novice or apprentice; and such is in truth his present *status*. The profane who seeks admission may be said to be a petitioner; during his initiation, he is a candidate; and when the initiation is completed, he is an Entered Apprentice. In the Old Regulations, *initiation* is held to be synonymous with *making a Mason*—that is, an Apprentice; and the rules that apply to the *makings*, as they are termed, refer only to the first degree: thus, the rule that a Lodge may not make more than five new brethren at the same time, means that not more than five persons may be initiated at the same meeting. The term "making" is never applied to the other degrees, in which the candidate is said to be *passed* or *raised*, as the case may be. While, therefore, initiation makes a man a Mason, it only confers upon him *a part* of the rights and benefits of the Lodge, the full privileges being reserved to the Master Masons.

An Entered Apprentice, not being a member, is not required to pay dues, and cannot make any claim upon the Lodge treasury; nor is his family, should he die before advancement, entitled to claim relief, as in the case of a member.

He may visit his own Lodge whenever opened on the first degree, but he has no voice or vote in the proceedings, nor can he serve on committees or hold office.

He cannot travel masonically, nor visit other Lodges, because he is not in possession of the means of making himself known as a member in good standing. Apprentices are sometimes allowed to visit other Lodges than their own, when accompanied and vouched by a Master Mason; but the practice is reprehensible, and ought not to be allowed. Instruction is due him in his own Lodge, and he should seek and find it there before going abroad.

He cannot, in case of death, be interred with the formalities of the institution; neither can he be allowed to take part in the procession on such occasions, the Lodge, when convened for that purpose, being always opened on the third or Master's degree.

He is particularly cautioned against entering into argument with the uninitiated, because, from his slight knowledge, he is unable to speak correctly of the society, and, in the heat of debate, may assert that which has no existence in fact.

He has the right to apply for instruction in the degree which has been conferred upon him, that, in due time, he may be prepared to advance another step in his profession.

He has the right to apply for the next or Fellow Craft degree,* but it does not follow that the Lodge is obliged to grant the request; for, in that case, the body could exercise no discrimination, and the rule which exacts suitable proficiency before advancement would be void. It is, therefore, the custom, when an Apprentice applies for the next higher degree, to require him to submit to an examination, either in open lodge or before a committee named for the purpose, that it may be known that he is prepared, by a knowledge of the degree already conferred, for advancement to another. When such examination is satisfactory, it is usual for the Lodge to express its willingness to advance him by a secret ballot, wherein one negative vote rejects him, without, however, affecting his standing as an Entered Apprentice. It is simply a refusal to allow him to advance, but in no wise interferes with his right to apply again.

We have known cases where, on the application of an Entered Apprentice for advancement, the negative ballot has been held to be an absolute rejection, as in the case of a profane, but there is a wide difference between the two. The question, on the ballot for advancement, is not whether the candidate shall be made a Mason, for that he already is, but simply

* Among French Masons, this is technically called "applying for higher wages."

whether he shall receive a higher degree, and, unless cause be shown to the contrary, an expression of opinion by the Lodge as to the proficiency already made. If a black ball appear, then some brother thinks the candidate has not sufficiently progressed in knowledge to be advanced, which opinion may be changed on another examination. But if it be held that such a ballot is an absolute rejection, then a Mason is condemned and executed—so to speak—without any semblance of a trial, without any charge being made, and without any proof being adduced. No such doctrine can be entertained. If there are reasons, other than want of proficiency, or, in other words, reasons affecting the moral character of the Apprentice, then, as a Mason, he has a right to a fair trial, that he may, if possible, exculpate himself, or, in the event of his failure to do so, that he may be placed in such position as will not only prevent his advancement, but forbid the exercise of his rights even as an Entered Apprentice. We say, then, that an Apprentice is entitled to a trial, but it must be understood that the trial is to be had before Master Masons, acting as a committee, that the accused may be present, and present his defence; the final decision will, however, be pronounced by the Lodge, opened in the third degree, where the Apprentice cannot enter.

Following this, is the right to appeal to the Grand Lodge for a review of the proceedings; for however limited the rights of an Entered Apprentice may be, he must be allowed their full enjoyment, and the use of all lawful means he may deem essential to their maintainance. Clearly, the right of appeal, after trial, is one that cannot be denied him.

In case of the removal of an Apprentice beyond the jurisdiction of the Lodge in which he was initiated, and on the expression of his wish to receive the remaining degrees at his new place of residence, the mother-lodge may furnish him a certificate, setting forth the fact of his regular initiation, together with its consent that he be advanced in the Lodge he may select.

In conclusion, it should be stated that in some Grand Lodge jurisdictions, laws prevail which are not in accordance with the views here given : in those jurisdictions, the local rule must be obeyed; but such cases are exceptions to the general law.

SECTION II.—FELLOW CRAFTS.

In former times, as will be seen by reference to the Ancient Charges and Regulations, Fellow Crafts were capable of being chosen Wardens of a Lodge, and even, at one time, Grand Master. That was when the majority of the Fraternity were Apprentices; but when the right to confer the second and third degrees was ceded to the Lodges by the Grand Lodge, and Master Masons took the place of the Apprentices, the rights previously enjoyed by Fellow Craft Masons disappeared, and they may now be said to have no rights beyond those of Apprentices, except that of applying for the third degree. They, therefore, occupy the same relation to a Master Mason that an Apprentice does to a Fellow Craft. They have the same disabilities as Apprentices, and are entitled to the same immunities. They are required to make suitable proficiency, and to serve some time before they can be raised to the degree of Master Mason.

The interval required to elapse between the degrees is not definitely, or rather not uniformly, settled. Some Grand Lodges require a month's probation between each degree; others more; some regulate the interval by "due proficiency." The Grand Lodge of New York requires proficiency, and that at least four weeks shall elapse between initiation and raising. In England the rule is twenty-eight days between each degree. It may, therefore, be said to be a matter of local regulation, as it certainly is subject to the control of the Grand Master, who may by his dispensation abbreviate, or entirely abrogate it.

SECTION IV.—MASTER MASONS.

Masons of the third degree of Ancient Craft Masonry now constitute the body of the Fraternity. They make up our Lodges, perform their labors, and contribute the means for paying their current expenses, as well as the demands of needy brethren, their widows and orphans. Their duties comprise the various requirements of the institution, and they are, in their generation, the custodians and conservators of the trust bequeathed by the fathers, which, in due time, they will leave to their sons, and thus perpetuate the institution while there shall remain a need for laborers in the cause of human progress. In view of the weighty responsibilities of Master Masons, it is proper that they should understand their rights and privileges, which we now proceed to enumerate.

The first right of a Master Mason is that of *membership*, which is of two kinds—actual and honorary. By actual membership is understood regular affiliation with a Lodge, either as the result of having been initiated, passed, and raised therein ; by acceptance, or affiliation after having been previously a member of some other Lodge, or by having been a member of a Lodge under dispensation, and remaining there after the warrant issues from the Grand Lodge.

It is always understood that when a person petitions for initiation in a Lodge, it is with the intention of becoming a member (unless the contrary be expressed), and therefore when the third degree has been conferred, no further ceremony is requisite save that of the candidate signing the by-laws, thus recording his willingness to assume his portion of the duties of Masonry, on condition that he be entitled to all the rights and benefits that accrue to members in good standing. This is the first method of obtaining membership. The second is when a Mason desires to change his membership from one Lodge to another ; he withdraws or dimits from his old Lodge and petitions the new one to receive him into fellowship. This petition takes the usual course ; a committee of investigation is named, and on their report a ballot is had, which, if favorable,* admits the petitioner to membership, on the condition of the fee as provided by the by-laws, and the appending his signature to that instrument. We digress here a moment to say, that among Masons in continental Europe the act of affiliation is always accompanied

* We have already remarked, in a previous chapter, that the ballot for an affiliating Mason differs from that for a profane in this, that if unfavorable his standing is not thereby affected. He is just as competent to petition the same Lodge, or another, after rejection as before, and that residence has nothing to do with the application unless ther) be a local regulation on the subject.

by appropriate ceremonies. The affiliating brother is required to renew his covenant of fealty to the constitution of the Grand Lodge, and to the regulations of the subordinate to which he is about to become attached. He is then introduced to the brethren by name, official announcement of his affiliation is made, and he is saluted as a member of the Lodge. The ceremony, though brief, is one that has always favorably impressed us, and we submit it to the consideration of the brethren. The third method of obtaining membership is where a given number of Master Masons petition the Grand Master to be formed into a Lodge under dispensation. Should their prayer be granted, it is the general rule that they must then withdraw from the old Lodge in which they had previously been members, membership in the new one accruing to them by their constitution under a warrant from the Grand Lodge, the risk of which they of course accept. In New York the rule is, that when Master Masons petition for a dispensation they must pay up their dues to the date of such petition and furnish satisfactory evidence of that fact to the Grand Master at the time of petitioning. If the dispensation be granted, the membership in the old Lodge remains in abeyance, and it is optional with the petitioners either to continue in the new Lodge when the warrant is granted, or to resume their membership in the old one. This rule is evidently fair and commendable, as it avoids the danger of setting men adrift who take part in the formation of new Lodges, in case the warrant of constitution does not follow the dispensation, and saves them the trouble and expense of a reäffiliation, in case they do not think proper to continue in the new Lodge.

Honorary membership, as generally understood, is the somewhat modern custom of conferring nominal membership on a brother for services rendered the Fraternity in general, or the Lodge in particular. As it is the law that a brother can only be an active member of one Lodge at the same time, and as only active members can participate in the transactions of the Lodge so far as to vote, hold office, serve on committees, etc., it follows that honorary membership when conferred is but the expression of a compliment, and that the honorary member acquires no positive right whatever. They are generally allowed to participate in discussion, but this is only an act of courtesy rarely denied to any visiting brother who signifies a wish to be heard.

There is, however, in some jurisdictions a kind of honorary membership which is positive and tangible in its operation. It is where, by the regulations of the Grand Lodge, a poor brother, unable to pay the adjoining fee, may be received by any Lodge without such fee, as an honorary member—by previous notice and unanimous ballot—and may be excused by the Lodge from the payment of dues. In this case the member is entitled to all the privileges of the Lodge, without being subjected to any of its pecuniary burdens.

From the right of membership follows the right to *visit* masonically any regular Lodge. There is considerable difference of opinion as to whether this is an absolute or limited right. The present Grand Master of England, and some authorities in this country, insist upon making the right to visit a positive one ; the only condition being, that the visiting brother shall produce satisfactory evidence of his good standing in the Lodge from which he hails. In this country, whatever the theory may be, the general practice is, however, to make the right a limited one. And we certainly must say that we can imagine no good reason for any other course. It is true that Lodges are in a general sense but the subdivisions of one universal family, but it must be admitted that the members of any particular Lodge have rights in it superior to the rights of Masons belonging to other Lodges, and when a member objects to the entrance of a visitor, his objection is, and ought to be, of greater weight than the claims of the visitor ; for if this were not the case the sitting member might be obliged to leave the Lodge, and thus be temporarily deprived of all his rights therein, at the order of a brother having equal rights in the Fraternity but not in the Lodge. Moreover, it is the duty of the Master to preserve harmony among the brethren composing his Lodge ; but if he were obliged to admit a visitor whose presence would, to his certain knowledge, disturb that harmony and embarrass the work, then he would be deprived of one of the means of performing an essential duty ; for peace and harmony are the support of our institution in a greater degree than in any other. Again, if the right to visit were a positive one, then Masons who believe ·that the landmark requiring candidates for Masonry to be free-born is still in force would be obliged to sit with a certain class of the initiates of a Grand Lodge which has unblushingly removed that landmark. Fortunately, however, the question is settled by the admitted prerogative of the Master to control the admission of visitors by withholding that permission, without which they can neither "pass nor repass."*

---

* Dr. OLIVER holds the right to visit to be absolute, but in the same breath admits that, under certain circumstances, visitors ought not to be admitted, or if present may be requested to withdraw, which sufficiently demonstrates the limited nature of the privilege.

In immediate connection with Masonic visitation
is the subject of certificates or diplomas.* Certificates being understood to emanate from a Lodge,
and diplomas from a Grand Lodge. There can be
no doubt of the right of a Master Mason in good
standing to furnish himself with a written proof of
that standing, vouched for by the seal of his Lodge,
or preferably his Grand Lodge, but little or no
weight can be given to such documents in the examination of a strange brother. They may be received
as collateral evidence, but the true dependence is the
Tyler's OB., the due trial and strict examination of a
competent and careful committee, who will omit no
question that ought to be asked, and who will accept
no equivocal answers; acting on the maxim that it
is better that ninety-nine good brethren should be
refused than that one impostor should be admitted.

The right of *avouchment* is a most important one,
and one in the exercise of which too much caution
cannot well be exercised. There are three rules in
regard to avouching, which may be thus stated :

1st. If you have been present in a regular Lodge
of Master Masons with the brother for whom you
vouch. 2nd. If a brother whom you *know* to be a
Master Mason introduces you to another *in person*,
and says I have sat with this brother ; or, 3d. If you,

* See Appendix.

as one of a committee appointed by the Master of your Lodge, have carefully examined a brother, then you may lawfully vouch for him, and your avouchment may be accepted by the Lodge. As a general rule, the personal examination of brethren casually meeting should not be accepted; for though there are undoubtedly many brethren just as competent to examine a stranger in any proper place as well as they could in the Lodge-room, yet the great majority are not thus competent, and it is therefore unsafe to accept such examinations and thus approve of the practice. Every Master has agreed in the most solemn manner that "no visitors shall be received in his Lodge without due examination and producing proper vouchers of their having been initiated in a regular Lodge," and he will prove faithless to his vow if he allow the somewhat loose system of modern avouchment to prevail under his administration. The simple announcement of "Brother so and so vouched for" is a very frail warrant for the admission of a person we have never seen or heard of before to a participation in our mysteries. We should know who is his sponsor, and on what grounds he assumes that responsibility. While it is the right of every Master Mason in good standing to vouch for another, on proper grounds, it is equally the duty of the Master to be satisfied that this important privi-

lege has not been lightly exercised, before he accepts
the voucher.   There are so many ways in which the
best intentioned brother may be deceived that there
should prevail a wholesome caution in accepting any
but the most irrefragible testimony.   Thus, the brother who offers to respond for another should know,
beyond all question, that the one he vouches for is
really a member of the Fraternity, in good standing,
and his knowledge must be obtained, not from an ordinary conversation nor a loose and careless inquiry,
but from strict trial, due examination, or lawful Masonic information, which one of the unwritten landmarks require as prerequisites to avouchment.   The
sixth subdivision of the sixth of the Ancient Charges
provides that—"You are cautiously to examine a
strange brother, in such a manner as prudence shall
direct you, that you may not be imposed upon by an
ignorant false-pretender, whom you are to reject with
contempt and derision, and beware of giving him
any hints of knowledge."   Nothing can lawfully be
taken for granted, nor should shortness of memory
be suffered to excuse the filling up of an inconvenient
blank.   If the would-be-visitor has paid so little heed
to his first instructions, or so little attention to the
claims of the Fraternity, as to become rusty, he should
go where he is known to obtain his information, and
be disappointed if he expect to pick it up from an

examining brother or committee. In this we would
be understood as referring to those important matters that are indispensible, and not to some of the
minor details that only a bright Mason could be expected to have at his finger-ends. The particulars
of an examination cannot, of course, be detailed here,
but we may say, in general terms, that the errors or
inadvertencies of the visitor should not be corrected,
for that would be giving him the hints we are warned
against. With an aged brother, or one who has long
been debarred the privileges of the Craft by journeys
or sickness, patience should be exercised. If he has
ever received the true light, the spark, though dimmed
will eventually brighten up by his own unaided endeavors ; and one such trial will always serve to remind him of the necessity of keeping his treasures
where he can find them when wanted. But it is not
so much from any carelessness in regard to examinations that we have to apprehend danger, as from the
uncertain application of what is termed "lawful information." The Tyler's voucher is very often an
uncertain guide ; for among the numbers that pass
his guard he may be deceived by great similarity of
personal appearance, or from a conviction that he,
having seen the person somewhere, that place must
have been in a Lodge ; or the Tyler may have known
that a person was a member of a Lodge, but not that

he had been put under discipline. Other instances might be named, but they will readily suggest themselves to the brethren. Examinations conducted by an inexperienced or unskillful brother can afford no just grounds for an avouchment, because he cannot be supposed to have the ability of detecting error, or the judgment necessary to avoid conveying information which should be withheld. If a brother vouch for another on the ground of having sat with him in Lodge, he should also be able to state positively that it was a Master's Lodge, duly and legally constituted, and not a Lodge of Entered Apprentices or Fellow Crafts. Written vouchers, though indited by your nearest friend, are of no positive value; they cannot lawfully contain any of those things which it is indispensible the visitor should know, and can afford him no assistance when put to the ordeal of strict examination. Personal avouchment from one brother to another may be accepted, but no further; and then only when the brother vouched for is in presence of the one giving the information and the one receiving it; and then it must be given with the intent of being used Masonically, and be full, explicit, positive, and based on actual knowledge of a Masonic character; but when Brother A informs Brother B that Brother C told him that Brother D was a Mason, the information becomes too loose to have a lawful value, and must be discarded. Finally, the safest and best rule for all concerned is for the visiting brother to be at the hall half an hour before the time fixed for Lodge opening, that he may have abundant time to prove his qualifications by the scrutiny of a regular examination.

The right to a *Masonic trial by his peers* is to the Mason, as to the citizen, the inviolable safeguard of all his other rights, and it is therefore an unchangeable law that the recognised punishments of Masonry can only be inflicted after a regular trial, during which, and until the final verdict is pronounced by the Lodge, he is entitled to the presumption of innocence, and remains in good standing. The method of proceeding in Masonic trials will form the subject of a separate and special consideration, and we therefore in this place only consider the right of every Mason to the benefit of such proceedings when by his conduct, or by the imputation of wrong, he becomes liable to impeachment. The enjoyment of the rights that inure to a Mason is that which distinguishes him from the profane, and entitles him to consideration among his brethren. Mere worldly justice, much more then, the sacred ties of the brotherhood, require that the penalties for immoral or unmasonic conduct should only be inflicted after trial, in which the charges shall have been sustained by ample proof, in which full opportunity shall have been afforded the accused to make his defence, and which proceedings shall have been approved by a majority of the brethren in open Lodge. The peers of a Master Mason are all other Master Masons in good standing in his Lodge, and therefore a Lodge has original jurisdiction for the purpose of trying any of its members save the Master, whose peers, while he remains in office, they are not, and whom, therefore, they cannot try.

The natural sequence of the right to a fair and impartial trial is the right of *appeal*. Human nature is fallible, and men, however just their intentions, are liable to err ; and it has therefore been provided that in all trials the accused brother shall have the right, when the Lodge has pronounced sentence, to appeal to the final adjudication of the Grand Lodge. The foundation of this right is found in the Sixth Charge, in these words : " If any complaint be brought, the brother found guilty shall stand to the award and determination of the Lodge, who are the proper and competent judges of all such controversies, unless you carry it by appeal to the Grand Lodge * * *." The requisites of an appeal (unless otherwise provided by the local regulations) are : 1st. That the appellant shall notify the opposite party of his intention to appeal. 2d.

That a copy of all the proceedings in the case, attested by the secretary and Lodge seal, shall be forwarded to the Grand Lodge without delay. 3d. That the appellant furnish the Grand Lodge, through the Grand Secretary, with a full and clear statement of the grounds of his appeal; and 4th. That a copy of this document be furnished to the adverse party. When a case is thus brought before the Grand Lodge, it is usually referred to a committee, who examine the papers, hear explanations from either or both parties, and report their judgment as to whether the proceedings ought to be reversed or confirmed, and on that report the Grand Lodge decides. Proceedings thus conducted are strictly appellate, but it is held that the Grand Lodge, being the supreme tribunal, may in its discretion assume original jurisdiction, hear new evidence, and make a new verdict. There is no doubt but that many Grand Lodges do thus act, but we must say that the power is one that ought not to be exercised except in an extreme case. The safer and just plan would seem to be, when there is manifest error in the proceedings, when the verdict is not in accordance with the evidence, or when the punishment awarded is too lenient or too severe, to send the case back for a new trial, with such recommendations as it may be proper to make, to the Lodge, who are " the

proper and competent judges in all such controversies."

Pending the appeal, the brother found guilty must
submit to the award of the brethren, so far as the
exercise of any of his Masonic rights, save that of
appeal, is concerned, because the Lodge having original jurisdiction had the right to pronounce sentence, which must therefore be in effect until absolutely reversed by the superior authority of the Grand
Lodge.   It may be objected, that in a case of definite suspension, say three or six months, the appellant would actually suffer the entire punishment before an appeal which might reverse the sentence
could be heard in Grand Lodge ; but of this there
is no real danger, for it cannot be doubted that during the recess of the Grand Lodge the Grand Master has ample power to entertain an appeal, and order a new trial if found necessary, or grant a stay of
proceedings until the assembling of the Grand
Lodge.

It is held, in a majority of the Grand Lodges of
this country, that where a Lodge has passed sentence
of indefinite suspension or expulsion—two names for
the same thing, in effect—though the Grand Lodge
may, on appeal, reverse the sentence for irregularity
or want of proof, it cannot and does not by such
reversal reinstate the member in his Lodge.   This

proposition is so diametrically opposed to common justice and common sense, that we trust to be excused for devoting a page or two to its consideration.

The object of the review by the Grand Lodge is to ascertain by impartial investigation that the proceedings have been regular, and that the finding is warranted by the evidence ; and until this conclusion is arrived at, the adjudication is not complete, and the accused brother remains so far connected with the institution (taking the supposition that the verdict was one of expulsion) as to have the right, by his appeal, to this final determination of the matter by the supreme tribunal. If the verdict of expulsion pronounced by the Lodge at once severs the connection of the individual with his Lodge and with the Fraternity, then all his Masonic rights are at once abrogated, and he could not enjoy the right of appeal, which is one of them. But the verdict of the Lodge is, and can only be, conditional, because the right of appeal is inalienable, and no brother can be deprived of it till his case has been finally reviewed and decided by the court of last resort. Hence, when a new trial is granted, a new appeal follows, just as if no previous trial had occurred. If, however, we admit the contrary view, then Masonic justice is a mockery, and the form of trial a solemn farce ; for if the reversal of the entire proceedings below does not place the brother in precisely the same situation he occupied before the charges were preferred, then all that is necessary to be done when a Lodge desires to get rid of a member is to trump up charges against him, declare him expelled, and, though the charges be false as the Father of lies, he is deprived of his membership beyond remedy ; and if the Grand Lodge, when upon examination it finds that the charges are unsustained, cannot reinstate him in all his rights, or rather cannot declare (and enforce its declaration) that he has not been deprived of any right, then it is lawful to vacate a brother's membership at will, and the right of appeal is no right, since it cannot procure the administration of the simplest form of justice. The advocates of this doctrine endeavor to justify it by saying that every Lodge is the judge as to who shall be its members, and that the Grand Lodge has no power to force any of its subordinates to accept a member against its will. As a general proposition, this is true ; but in the case of a reversal of judgment the Grand Lodge does nothing like forcing a member upon the Lodge ; it simply says : "We have examined your record ; we find your proceedings wrong, and that the evidence you have furnished us does not establish the charges made ; they are therefore null and void ;"

and the result is to restore the state of things that existed before proceedings were commenced ; and hence the brother *continues* the membership, of which, by the reversal of the sentence, it is declared he had not been deprived.

Appeals from other acts and decisions of the Lodge besides those relating to trials are sometimes taken. Appeals from the decision of the Master in the chair are likewise to be made to the Grand Lodge or Grand Master—usually to the latter, or to his deputy, for the reason that they generally involve some point or principle which it is necessary to the harmony of the Lodge should be decided without delay. This appeal is the safeguard of the member against any exercise of arbitrary authority by the Master, and the "check" by which he is restrained from the use of his high prerogatives to the injury of the Lodge or the brethren.

The right of *relief*, when in circumstances of destitution and distress, is one of the most ancient and well-established rights of the individual Mason. It existed before the constitution of permanent Lodges, and before the institution of the Grand Lodge. It has in modern times been modified in the case of non-affiliated Masons, but otherwise remains as in the beginning ; for a Mason has a claim not only to the benevolence of the particular Lodge of which he

9

is a member, but upon that of the whole Fraternity
wherever dispersed ; a claim, too, that after his death
inures to his widow and children. Relief as now
given may be said to be of two kinds : personal, that
is, donations from individual resources to relieve a
destitute brother ; and, from the funds of the Lodge
or Grand Lodge, for a like purpose. In the present
day, when there is a Lodge in every village in the
land, it appears to us that the claim upon individual
members ought not to be enforced ; for the tax is in
many instances beyond the ability of the brother, especially if he be well known, or live in the vicinity of
persons inimical to the institution. Money contrib-
uted to the Lodge fund is deposited for the very
purpose of relief, and every contributor ought to be
allowed to refer applicants to it, unless, of course,
where he is persuaded that it is a duty to give from
his own pocket, as well as from the Lodge treasury.
We speak on this topic from an extended personal
experience, and from actual knowledge that the be-
nevolent feature of the Masonic association has been,
and will be, liable to great abuse ; for on it has grown
that unsightly parasite Masonic vagrancy. To a su-
perficial observer, it would seem that our system was
expressly intended to provide against mendicancy in
any shape, and that our professions of benevolence
are but hollow shams, while we allow our own kin-

dred and people to fall into the vicious state of professional beggars; but those who are in the habit of looking beyond the surface need not be told, that Masonry does not pretend to be an eleemosynary establishment; that it is rather a system of morality, one of the duties of which is, to relieve the distresses of its worthy adherents, and those of their widows and orphans; or, in other words, that charity, or the giving of alms, is but an adjunct to other and more important duties. Saith the law: "If thy brother be waxen poor, and fallen into decay with thee, then thou shalt relieve him; yea, though he be a stranger or a sojourner; that he may live with thee." (Leviticus xxv., 35.) And it truly describes the real purpose of Masonic donations. For this purpose our members cheerfully impose upon themselves a tax which, as citizens, they would not submit to without murmuring, and the proceeds of which they give with a liberal hand, not only to the "brother waxen poor" among us, and those who have a natural right to ask in his name, but also, in too many cases, to those who neither have, nor ought to have, a claim upon anything but the way to the door.

This is a defect of our present administration of charity that is daily working evil not only to the Craft, but to the recipients themselves; for we hold that money given to the idle and viciously disposed, not only does wrong to the giver, but also to the recipients, as they are thus encouraged not only to continue a life of idleness, but to exercise their wits for new methods of imposing on the too credulous stewards of a fund intended for a far different purpose. The practice of benevolence is often and strongly inculcated in our ritual, in monitors, and in all publications which undertake to treat of Masonry; but it is in almost every case taken literally, and without consideration as to what true benevolence is. We say that the mere giving of money is not charity, for charity implies love, and requires discrimination. Our gifts, unlike the gentle dew of heaven, should not fall alike on the just and the unjust; for vice, like noxious weeds, grows rampant enough without fertilizing. Add this consideration : that every dollar misgiven to an impostor is two dollars taken from the true claimant, and a sufficient reason will be found for the exercise of greater caution than seems to prevail among the Lodges of our country. While, therefore, we would applaud the liberal assistance given to those *known* to be worthy, we would equally condemn that loose giving that merely requires the presentation of a doubtful paper and a plausible story to unloose the purse-strings. We do not speak unadvisedly when we thus characterise a process vastly too common to be either denied or suffered to continue without expostulation. We do not for a moment call in question the intention of those who so freely give the Lodge means to applicants, but we warn them that they cannot thus discharge the trust reposed in them, nor be certain that in thus giving they are in reality assisting the meritorious; that, on the contrary, they thus in many instances furnish the means for idleness and dissipation, and in the same proportion deprive themselves of the pleasure they might otherwise enjoy in giving more generously to those whose right is undisputed.

We hold that even in the latter case there is more than money required in the fulfillment of our duty. Money will often cut the knot of a difficulty which it were better to spend a little time in untying. A word in season to the desponding, or of encouragement to those honestly striving, may produce more lasting benefit than any amount of money could do without them. "Words fitly spoken are like apples of gold in pictures of silver." How often have such words enlivened the gloom of affliction and converted the night of despair into the morning of joy! How have they reclaimed the wanderer from the paths of vice, and shielded the unfortunate from the shafts of malice and oppression! Yet how often is their value lost, and conscience silenced, by adding an extra dollar or so to the appropriation?

To be entitled, therefore, to ask relief, a Mason must not only be in real need, but he must be worthy and under the general ruling, a member of some Lodge ; for one of the disabilities of non-affiliated Masons is, that they have no claim on the benevolence of the Fraternity. Where the application is made by the widow, or in behalf of orphan children, it is required that proper documentary evidence be furnished that the applicants are entitled to claim relief in the name of a deceased brother. There can be no question that when the widow of a deceased Mason marries a second time she loses all claims upon the Fraternity accruing from the membership of her first husband. The minor children are, however, regarded as still having a claim.

In connection with this topic, the establishment of Lodges, or Boards of Relief, presents itself ; but as their management is purely one of convenience, and subject to no law but what the brethren controlling them may see proper to enact, it is out of place in this Treatise. We, however, warmly approve of and earnestly recommend them to the Craft of all large cities and towns, as having proved the best safe-guards against impostors, and the best defence of the worthy distressed.

The right to *withdraw from membership*, or, as it is technically called, to dimit, is one that leads to great differences of opinion. The law of 1721, that "No set or number of brethren shall withdraw or separate themselves from the Lodge in which they were made brethren, or were afterwards admitted members, unless the Lodge become too numerous," evidently does not apply to the occasional withdrawal of individuals, because in addition to the term "set or number of brethren" it is required that the withdrawal should only take place when the Lodge becomes too numerous; that it should be for the purpose of forming a new Lodge, and that such purpose should have the sanction of the Grand Master or his Deputy, by the issue of his dispensation to form such new Lodge. This was evidently to guard against the possibility of a number of the brethren, under the influence of sudden passion, withdrawing from a Lodge, and perhaps breaking it up. And though the same purpose might be accomplished by the withdrawing of one individual after another, there is at all events a better opportunity for reason and a sense of duty to resume their sway, than if the majority should be allowed to dimit at once. This is, however, an extreme case, hardly likely to occur, because the majority would have the right to control the affairs of the Lodge, and direct its legislation to suit their own views.

We refer to the right of an individual Mason, for

reasons of his own, to sever his connection with the
Lodge of which he may be a member, and we fail to
discover any general law to prevent it, except that
the dimitting member shall be clear of the books—
that is, have paid all indebtedness to the Lodge, and
that there be no charges against him pending at the
time of such dimission. Such has been the custom
in this country from the the first introduction of Masonry into it till within a few years. Various attempts
have been made to put a stop to the evil of non-affiliation; first, by attaching disabilities to that condition, and then by requiring the withdrawing member
to obtain the consent of his Lodge, in addition to the
requirements above stated. The argument is, that
as the consent of the Lodge is required for the admission of a member, so it should be necessary to
the severance of that connection. Speaking of this
argument, a distinguished Craftsman has well said :
"The theory here laid down may be one which commends itself to favorable consideration, but I feel
constrained to say that, in practice, it is not entitled
to the same regard. I can see no valid reason why
a brother in good standing, if not a Master or Warden, who has discharged all his pecuniary obligations to his Lodge, and so long as he leaves members
enough to form a working Lodge, should not be permitted to dimit of his own volition, and without tak-

ing any vote whatever on the subject. Many things might be said which would sustain this view, but I will only cite a single case. It is impossible to enforce the regular attendance of a member of a Lodge who has been foiled in his effort to withdraw from it, except by the service of a summons upon him previously to each communication. Even that compulsory process might be evaded by a brother, if he should so choose, without making him liable to the infliction of any penalty. We will suppose that such a brother had conscientious scruples, which, if disclosed, would involve the honor of his family, against associating with a member of his Lodge ; or suppose any other cause to exist, leading to the same result, what becomes the necessary effect of this? The brother either suffers his name to be struck from the roll for non-payment of dues, or pays dues for privileges which he cannot conscientiously enjoy, and avoids attendance on his Lodge. Hence it is that the Craft loses the services of a good member, and virtually puts him out of the pale of association of a Lodge which he can call his own, by preventing his affiliation with one more congenial to his taste, or his sense of propriety. I can see no good reason why we should not return to the voluntary system, under which we very happily worked in years past."*

* M. W. John J. Crane, M.D. ; annual address to the Grand Lodge of New York, 1863.

As it is undoubtedly true, that a brother kept in affiliation with his Lodge is only a nominal member, and can be of no earthly use beyond the amount of dues he may contribute, we think, with the brother just quoted, that the interests of all parties would be best served by leaving each member to change his affiliation, or even to incur the odium of non-affiliation, when he can no longer maintain the emulation as to who can " best work" and who " best agree." But if we admit the right of a brother in good standing to withdraw at pleasure, we cannot deny that the granting of a certificate of that fact is a legislative act which the Lodge may or may not do. Without that certificate the brother cannot affiliate elsewhere, for it is the general sense of the Craft that no Lodge can affiliate a member unless he be able to show that he has honorably withdrawn from the Lodge to which he last belonged, and that evidence is the dimit.* It is therefore most masonic and fraternal that the severance of membership should be a matter of mutual understanding ; that the brother should understand that if he withdraw in the heat of passion, or against the sense of the brethren, he incurs the risk of losing the document necessary to his admission elsewhere ; and, on the other hand, that the Lodge, when a brother in good standing desires to withdraw, and a

* See Appendix.

fraternal remonstrance fails to change his purpose, should allow him to consummate his purpose, and afford him the requisite facility for an affiliation that may be more convenient or agreeable to him. It will be understood that where there is a local regulation it will necessarily govern any action that may be proposed or taken.

Where a vote is taken on an application for a dimit, and carried in the affirmative, it cannot be reconsidered, for the reason that by the announcement of its passage the member at once becomes non-affiliated ; and though he might instantly repent of his application, he can only regain his lost membership by petition and a unanimous ballot in his favor. A dimit must be applied for in person, or if in writing, then over the proper signature of the brother desiring it. The act cannot be accomplished through a third party, for evident reasons.

Lastly, a Master Mason who dies in good standing has a right to *burial* with the ancient formalities of the institution. The earliest authority we find upon this subject is that of Preston, who says : " No Mason can be interred with the formalities of the Order unless it be at his own special request, communicated to the Master of a Lodge of which he died a member ; foreigners and sojourners excepted ; nor unless he has been advanced to the third degree of Mason-

ry, from which restriction there can be no exception.
Fellow Crafts or Apprentices are not entitled to the
funeral obsequies." As the first edition of Preston's
Illustrations, from which this extract is taken, was
published in 1772, it is questionable whether the ceremony at funerals, and the regulations concerning
them, were very much older than Preston himself.
They are now, however, universally obeyed, and the
exhortation at the grave, written by him, is substantially that in use throughout the United States. It
is now held that none but affiliated Masons, except
foreigners or sojourners, have a right to masonic
burial; and hence, that non-affiliated Masons cannot
be thus interred, which is in accordance with the
regulation quoted; for the request must have been
preferred to the Lodge of which the brother died a
member. In the case of a member who dies in good
standing, but without making such request, the funeral honors are generally accorded to his remains
at the request of his family or near relatives.

It was a rule in Preston's time, that there should
be no funeral or other public procession in the badges
and insignia of masonry, without a dispensation had
first been obtained from the Grand Master or his
Deputy; and the avowed object of the regulation
was to prevent the too frequent appearance of the
brethren in public, and that, too, on occasions not

likely to advance the cause of Masonry, or enhance its position in the public estimation. For like reasons a similar rule prevails in nearly every Grand Lodge jurisdiction in this country, though the law is generally more stringent in large cities than in the rural districts, where there is less liability to abuse.

A proper regard for the proprieties of a funeral solemnity requires that the brethren should wear dark clothing, and leave at home all Masonic decorations but plain white aprons, white gloves, and the sprig of evergreen.

SECTION V.—NON-AFFILIATED MASONS.

By non-affiliated Masons is understood those brethren who have received the several degrees of symbolic Masonry, but who are not attached to any Lodge, which, previous to the revival of 1717, was the status of the whole Craft; when, as we understand it, Lodges were distinguished by their place of meeting : as, those at the Goose and Gridiron, in St. Paul's churchyard; the Crown, in Parker's lane, near Drury lane ; the Apple-tree Tavern, in Charles street, Covent Garden ; the Rummer and Grapes Tavern, in Channel-row, Westminster, etc., rather than by any permanent or continuous organization, and a Mason was a member of the Lodge he happened to attend ; but since that time it is held that a brother ought to belong to some Lodge and be subject to its by-laws and the General Regulations. There is, however, a large number (comparatively speaking) of unaffiliated Masons who are believed to be able to bear their proportion of the general burden, but who in a great measure escape it by neglecting or refusing to keep up membership in a Lodge. This is felt to be so great an injustice, that in many jurisdictions it is called a Masonic crime, and many Grand Lodges have sought to punish it as such—attempts which have thus far been but moderately successful ; principally because there has been no unity of action or sentiment on the question, a result in a great measure due to a foolish spirit of exclusiveness, which prevents Grand Lodges from mutual consultation and action on subjects in which all alike are interested. Some of the legislation, too, has been of a character to effect the very reverse of what was intended. Men will not always be forced to do right ; on the contrary, the very effort to do so produces, in a majority of cases, an aggravation of the evil sought to be remedied.

Certain disabilities are, however, now admitted to be the consequence of non-affiliation, and Masons thus situated are, it is agreed :

Not entitled to claim relief from the funds of the Lodge or Grand Lodge.

Not entitled to visit any Lodge more than twice while they remain non-members.

Not entitled to join in Masonic processions.

Not entitled to the honors of Masonic burial.

They nevertheless remain subject to the general rules of the Fraternity, and may be tried and punished for an infraction of them by any Lodge within the jurisdiction of which they may happen to be.

They may, when in true and imminent danger, ask assistance in the usual method, and a Mason must respond, because in such case he cannot stop to ask questions, which might also be the case with an expelled or suspended brother.

Whenever the Craft generally unite in considering a non-contributing drone as no Mason, and refuse him the privileges of the Lodge, except one visit to enable him to select one in which he can affiliate, the number will grow less; but while, as at present, they are frequently allowed to visit the same Lodge many times, it is probable that the army of those who begrudge the pittance necessary to maintain active membership will continue to increase.

CHAPTER VII.

The Penal Code.

IF any one were disposed to claim for Masonry, or for Masons, anything not rightfully belonging to humanity, and subject to its frailties and short-comings, the caption of this chapter ought to dispel the illusion. It is at once an acknowledgment of our fallibility and an assurance that, recognizing the infirmities of human nature, we have prepared to deal with the erring, not harshly, nor at the behest of arbitrary will, but firmly, mercifully, and in the spirit of impartiality ; meting out justice to the guilty without fear or favor, but governing our investigations by that charitable principle of the common law which regards every man as innocent till he is fairly proved guilty. This was not always so ; for the period is not very far in the past when it was held that, as a Mason's reputation, like that of the Roman matron, should be above suspicion, so the very fact of charges being preferred against him was the signal for his loss of caste, and he was called to prove his innocence before his guilt had been established. So monstrous a proposition carried with it its own condemnation, and in the more just and liberal views that now prevail we see that while the world moves Masonry moves with it. It is a matter of frequent complaint, that the administration of the penal laws of Masonry is too complicated for the general comprehension, and that, with the aid of a lawyer, even the guilty may escape merited punishment. There is not, however, sufficient ground for the complaint; for in our somewhat extensive experience in such matters we have not met with such a case. We *have* known instances where the brethren, feeling a moral certainty that an accused brother was guilty, have murmured because they were not allowed to declare him so, in the absence of all legal proof! And the brother acting as counsel has been severely and unjustly criticised for standing between his client and any such unlawful conclusion. It is a very common mistake of men unused to legal proceedings, to adopt the convictions of their own minds as to the guilt of a brother under charges, without any regard to the production of such evidence as would lead a totally unbiased person to the same conclusion; and these are the ones most likely to regard the forms of law as irksome and intricate, because apparently delaying a decision to which they arrive without any form at all. We need not detain the reader with argument to refute so untenable a position, but content ourselves with saying, for the sake of many good brethren who do not seem to comprehend the value of judicial proceedings, that the rights of a Mason are sacred ; that he not only has a right to their enjoyment, but a claim to the assistance and protection of all other Masons in maintaining them ; and hence, that he can only be deprived of them on the clearest proof, and being afforded every fair opportunity to establish his defence.

The Penal Code of Masonry has three divisions : Masonic Offences, Masonic Trials, and Masonic Punishments ; connected with which is the subject of Restoration. We will notice them in the order here named.

SECTION I.—MASONIC OFFENCES.

The first of the Ancient Charges informs us, that : " A Mason is obliged, by his tenure, to obey the moral law ;" and this may be said to be the key to all the requirements for the conduct of the brethren. The moral law is the first of all laws, because it includes the law of God, and to violate one is to violate both. The rights and benefits of Masonry are conferred on a profane, under the belief that he has a good moral character and standing in the community, and that the manner of life which has acquired such a character for him will be continued when, having been admitted to the Fraternity, he shall become an exemplar of its teachings. It is on this condition, or as it is technically called, " tenure," that he is permitted to enter the Temple ; on it that he is allowed to enjoy the privileges of the Craft and claim its protection when needed ; by his observance of it that he can really say that he is a Mason, or that he can be qualified to sit in judgment on his brethren who yield to temptation. And therefore we say, that an offence against the moral law is an offence against Masonry ; for Masonry is, and from the very nature of its constitution can only be, a system of morality. It therefore follows, that a Mason who indulges in the vices of profane swearing, habitual intoxication, or others that subject him to contempt, and bring shame and disgrace upon the Fraternity, represented in his person, or who wilfully violates the solemn sanctions of his covenants, is a Masonic offender. Some of these offences are naturally more venial than others, and subject to a much less penalty on conviction, and in those cases it is held that the discipline of the Craft cannot be exercised till the offender has been admonished by the Master or Wardens, as provided in the ninth of the Regulations of 1721. We regard this as a very important rule, not only as being in the oldest written law, but because it exemplifies the spirit of Masonry, which, like true charity, is long-suffering and kind, and seeks to exhaust the influences of brotherly love before resorting to sterner proceedings.

There are offences against the moral law which are so heinous in their nature that to dally with them by remonstrance or admonition would almost be to approve them ; in such cases, proceedings should be instituted and carried to conclusion without other than the necessary legal delay.

Violations of the Masonic law—as, wilful disobedience of the constitution or the by-laws of a Lodge ; Masonic intercourse with a clandestine Lodge or Mason, or with a suspended or expelled brother ; defrauding a brother Mason ; embezzling the funds of the Lodge or Grand Lodge ; violating the unwritten landmarks ; refusing obedience to the lawful commands of a Masonic superior ; wilfully neglecting or refusing to obey a summons, are offences in Masonry which subject the offender to punishment of greater or less severity, according to the circumstances of the case. In all these instances, and many others that might be enumerated, a discreet Master will mark out a course to be pursued with greater accuracy than could be accomplished by any general rule we could frame.

Violating the law of the land is necessarily a Masonic offence, because the offender in disgracing himself also disgraces the Fraternity, the whole Craft receiving blame for the acts of the individual. In such a case, charges are to be preferred as though no trial had taken place before the civil tribunal; but it is not necessary that all the evidence should be repeated. The testimony of two brethren who were present at the civil trial, and who certify the general tenor of the evidence, will be sufficient; or, where the accused is already convicted of a felony, the official record of such conviction will be sufficient evidence for the prosecution.

In dealing with such cases, a distinction is to be made between felonies and misdemeanors. Felonies entail personal disgrace and loss of character, while misdemeanors may be the simple neglect of a corporation ordinance entailing a trivial fine. The best of men may be convicted of such an offence without disgrace.

Political offences cannot be made the subject of Masonic discipline, because Masonry takes no cognizance of political differences. "So that if a brother should be a rebel against the State, he is not to be countenanced in his rebellion, however he may be pitied as an unhappy man; and if convicted of no other crime, though the loyal brotherhood must and ought to disown his rebellion and give no umbrage or ground of political jealousy to the government for the time being, they cannot expel him from the Lodge, and his relation to it remains indefeasible."*

Religious differences, especially in countries where ecclesiastical powers are recognized by the State, are subject to the like rule for similar reasons.

SECTION II.—MASONIC TRIALS.

In the whole range of Masonic topics, there is none more difficult to deal with than the one we now propose to examine; not so much from any inherent difficulty in the subject itself, as because it is one about which the generality of the Craft know little or nothing, and (in one sense it may be said) fortunately have little opportunity to acquire knowledge. For when a trial takes place, it is usually confined to the Lodge having jurisdiction, visitors being, very properly, excluded; and thus many of the brethren know nothing of the forms usual to such occasions. The judicial powers of a Lodge are, however, a part of its well-established prerogatives, and it is proper that their intention should be understood, as well as the forms by which they are accomplished.

In a majority of Grand Lodge jurisdictions, trials are held in open Lodge; but as in many cases it is necessary for committees to be appointed to take the

* Ancient Charges, Art. II.

evidence of persons who could not be present to testify, it will, we think, eventually be the general rule
to name committees to take all the evidence during
the recess of the Lodge, and present that evidence,
with the conclusions of the committee, to the Lodge
for its final action.   Such is the practice in the State
of New York, and we shall here follow that model
not only for the sake of perspicacity, but in the hope
that a knowledge of its advantages may lead to its
general adoption.   The forms used we have placed
in the Appendix, for the convenience of Lodges where
they are the law, and for the examination of brethren
elsewhere.   The object of Masonic trials, like all others, is to demonstrate the guilt or innocence of the
brother under charges, by the testimony of competent
witnesses, before an unbiased tribunal, where everything may be done in a regular and orderly manner,
and where there may be as absolute certainty as the
imperfection of human nature will admit, that impartial justice will be awarded ; the accused being entitled to the presumption of innocence till proved
guilty, and the accuser to purity of motive and sincerity of purpose.   Trials occur either as the result
of an accusation against a brother for unmasonic
conduct, or to determine controversies between
Lodges or individuals.

The first step in a Masonic trial is the presentation

of charges, which must be done in open Lodge, at a stated communication by a brother in good standing (usually the Junior Warden), non-affiliated Masons and profanes not being competent to prefer charges.

The charges must be in writing, and must fully specify the offence charged, together with the time and place of its commission, and must be signed by the accuser, even when presented by the Junior Warden. The indictment is read in open Lodge by the Secretary, and the Lodge decides by vote whether the charges shall be accepted and the accused brother be placed on trial. When decided in the affirmative, the Master appoints a commission of three, five or more members, to hear, try and determine the same.

The next step is the service of the charges, which is done by the Secretary furnishing a copy certified by the Lodge seal, which, together with a summons directing the delinquent to appear at a time and place therein named, with his witnesses, for the purpose of trial, is personally served on him, or left at his residence or place of business.

The time allowed between the service of charges and the trial varies according to circumstances. Where the accused is a resident of the place in which the Lodge is held, ten days are generally deemed sufficient, though, for cause shown, a further reasonable delay will always be granted. When the accused resides more than twenty miles from the Lodge, service is allowed by mail, and twenty or thirty days are given, and longer time when at a greater distance and out of the State. If the residence be unknown, or the delinquent has absconded, the Lodge may proceed *ex parte* and conduct the case as though the delinquent were present. When the summons is disobeyed, then another is issued and served, citing the accused to show cause why he should not be disciplined for such contempt, and in the event of continued neglect, the committee may either report judgment for contempt, or proceed to hear the evidence as in the case of an absconding member.

On receipt of the charges, the defendant should, previous to the time named for the trial, make answer to them in writing, in which he may either simply plead not guilty, or admit a portion and deny the rest of the specifications, as to him may seem proper. The object of this is to save time in the investigation by reducing the facts requiring proof to the narrowest possible limits, and to avoid all extraneous matters tending to complicate the trial. This suggestion will be found of great convenience in controversies between individuals or Lodges, or where charges are preferred against a Master by his Lodge, as affording an opportunity for explanation and a possibility

10

of mutual arrangement, which ought always to be the first aim of all concerned.

Where controversies arise between Lodges, or between individuals or the members of different Lodges, the general custom is for the trial to be had in or by the Lodge to which the member belongs against whom charges are first made ; but though we are not prepared to say that a fair trial may not be thus obtained, there is nevertheless in such a course an apparent want of that strict impartiality which is at the very foundation of justice. It therefore appears fairer that such complaints, as well as those against Masters of Lodges, should be made to the Grand Lodge, or its officers charged with that duty, and that they should select commissioners from among the Masters and Wardens of neighboring Lodges admittedly free from all bias in the premises. When charges are thus preferred, the commission make their report to the Grand officer appointing them, and their judgment is final, unless the proceedings be found irregular and a new trial be ordered, or an appeal be made to the Grand Lodge. In the latter case, the delinquent remains under effect of the sentence till it is legally reversed.

At any time before the trial, the defendant may offer objections to the commissioners, on the score of bias, and when this happens they should either resign, or be removed by the appointing power, or triers be appointed and the defendant be allowed an opportunity to show cause. These things would be allowed a defendant in civil law. How much more ought it to be done when the reputation of a brother is at stake.

All the preliminaries having been adjusted, the commission meet at the time and place named in the summons and organize by the appointment of one of their number chairman, and a clerk, who need not necessarily be a commissioner. The defendant is then admitted with his counsel, if he have one. Any Master Mason in good standing may act as such counsel, but not a profane. The charges and specifications are read, and the case is then open. At this period the defendant may offer in writing any objections he thinks proper to make, to the jurisdiction of the Lodge, to the defective nature of the specifications or others. The commission will decide as to their validity. If the points of objection are found to be well taken, it would be useless to proceed further, because there would be a reasonable certainty that on appeal the proceedings would be reversed. If, on the contrary, they be deemed invalid, and the commission so decide, a note to that effect is entered on the minutes, and a copy of the paper is filed with the clerk as a part of the case. It would, however, be better, as we have already observed, that all such objections should be made in the written answer of the defendant to the charges, to be served on the commission as soon after the reception of the charges as possible, that the commissioners may have ample time to consider them before making a decision.

The examination of witnesses (who are to be called before the commission, one at a time,) will now take place; first, in behalf of the prosecution, and then for the defence. And here we may devote a moment to inquire who may be witnesses on a Masonic trial.

Children of tender years, unable to comprehend the solemnity of an obligatian; persons of unsound mind, atheists; persons who have been convicted of heinous crimes, and expelled Masons, are incompetent to testify. In addition to these, it should be the rule, although it is not always, that persons interested in the result of the trial—that is, persons whose interests would be affected, either favorably or unfavorably, by the result—should not be allowed to testify. Masons wives are generally allowed to give evidence on the trial of their husbands, when desired to do so; but we think the practice an unsafe one, and one that ought to be guided by the rule in civil law which forbids such testimony. Women not thus interested, and profanes, may give evidence before a commission, but where the trial is in open Lodge, they would have to be examined by a committee named for the purpose, and in presence of the accused, who has the right to propound cross-interrogatories, and who would accompany the committee for that purpose.

Lodge-books and vouchers, and certified extracts therefrom, are occasionally and properly introduced as testimony.

Master Masons in good standing are of course competent witnesses, and give their testimony under the sanction of their covenants, the commission having no power to administer judicial oaths, and not being allowed to do so if they had.

The accused has the right to cross-examine all witnesses.

The general rules of evidence apply in Masonic trials, but not all. For instance, where a brother is charged with habitual intoxication no evidence can be introduced tending to convict him of fraud, or any other crime; nor would it be proper to attempt to elicit such information on the examination of a witness placed on the stand to substantiate the charge of intoxication. This is one of the errors into which brethren unaccustomed to legal proceedings are most likely to be led; and more judgments are reversed on such grounds than almost any other. No attempt should, therefore, be made to prove anything not laid down in the charges.

The questions asked, and the answers given by the witnesses, are to be written down *verbatim* by the clerk—first the direct, and then the cross-examination ; and when the deposition of a witness is concluded, it should be read over to him, and he should approve its correctness by appending his signature to it.

Hearsay evidence cannot be admitted ; the witnesses must be able to testify of his own knowledge, or not at all.

A Master Mason cannot be impeached. He may be contradicted by the introduction of witnesses to prove a contrary state of facts to that alleged by him, but no witnesses can be allowed to testify that they would not believe him under oath, as is frequently done in civil suits. If a Mason has so far lost his character as to be unworthy of belief, even when testifying under oath, there must be some cause for it, and he should therefore be put under charges, tried, and excluded from the Craft ; but until these things have been done, he is entitled to the considerations attaching to regular standing.

Lastly, the object of a Masonic trial is to ascertain the exact truth in regard to a charge preferred, that strict justice may govern the administration of discipline. No mere technicality ought to be allowed to stand in the way of producing the necessary facts,

and when such technicalities are insisted upon by
counsel, the better way would be to note the objection on the minutes, produce the facts, and leave the
decision to the appellate tribunal. A Mason accused
of delinquency ought to depend on an open rebuttal
of the accusation, and not upon the skilful handling
of what, in common parlance, we term "legal quib-
bles." During a somewhat extended observation of
Masonic trials, we have always found that, as the
committees are usually plain men, unacquainted with
the technicalities and subtleties of law proceedings,
so a plain, straight-forward course is the most likely
to be successful ; and, indeed, it would be a scandal
to Masonry were the facts otherwise, for if a guilty
brother may avoid conviction by an authorized resort to the chicanery of the law, then, by a parity of
reasoning, an innocent one might be convicted by a
similar process. To admit either proposition would
be to degrade Masonry, by assimilating it to the unfair practices of the world, and taking from its arcana
the cardinal virtues which are at the foundation of
its system. We shall not be misunderstood as ob-
jecting to the employment of counsel in Masonic investigations, for we favor such a course, on the ground
that, being disinterested, they are not affected by the
passions of the immediate litigants ; and further, that
by their knowledge they are enabled to avoid unnec-

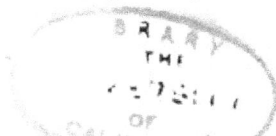

essary circumlocution, **thus** keeping the proceedings within due bounds ; but we do object, and we warn the brethren — both lay and professional—against making the result of Masonic trials dependent upon the subtleties by which reputations and fortunes are won or lost in the lottery of common law.

The evidence being all in, it is then optional with the parties concerned to sum up. We have only to say, in this regard, that never having known a summing up to have the slightest effect upon the result, we leave it as a matter of taste to those concerned.

If the proceedings have been lengthy, the commission usually have a meeting by themselves to read over the evidence and agree as to their conclusion, a majority of the commission being required to find a verdict. Having settled upon their verdict, the clerk is directed to notify the accused of that fact, and that the commission will present their conclusions to the Lodge at its next stated communication. At that communication the report is presented and read, together with the evidence, if required, and the Lodge then proceeds to consider the question : " Shall the finding of the commissioners be approved ?" Debate is allowed, and the defendant or his counsel may be heard. The Lodge may in its discretion alter, approve, or reverse the finding. Before taking the vote, however, the accused is directed to retire, and then the Lodge finally passes upon the case,* subject, of course, to an appeal, of which the accused is expected to give notice within such time as may be fixed by the regulations.

Where, as under certain circumstances provided in the constitution of the Grand Lodge of New York,† the commission is appointed by the Grand Master, the report is made to him, and his approval makes it final, unless appeal be taken to the Grand Lodge within six months. Where the Deputy, or one of the District Deputies, names the commission, report is made to the appointing officer, but appeal may be taken to the Grand Master, and again to the next succeeding Grand Lodge.

SECTION III.—MASONIC PUNISHMENTS.

The penalties inflicted for Masonic offences are: Reprimand; Exclusion, which is temporary or permanent; Suspension, definite or indefinite; and Expulsion. In England, fines are permitted to be levied

* The manner of voting, on these occasions, differs in the various Grand Lodge jurisdictions. In some it is required to be taken by ballot. In others, *viva voce*; and in others it is left to the discretion of the Lodges.

† Controversies between Lodges, or between individuals belonging to different Lodges, or where charges are preferred against the Master of a Lodge.

under the name of punishments; but the sentiment of the American Fraternity being decidedly averse to them, they are held among us to be unmasonic.

Reprimand is the mildest form of Masonic punishment, and, though it can only be inflicted after trial, is considered rather as an admonition to the offender for some trifling breach of the law, and as a notice of intention to preserve intact the dignity of our profession.

This punishment should, when possible, be administered by the Master in person, and be made the occasion for reminding, not only the delinquent, but the brethren generally, of the sacred nature of our engagements, and the certainty that they cannot be violated with impunity.

Exclusion, when temporary in its effect, is administered by the Grand Master, in the Grand Lodge, for refusal to submit to the rules of order, contumacy to the authority of the Grand Master, or, in brief, for any conduct not sufficiently heinous to call for indictment and trial, but too much so to be allowed to pass without notice.

The same thing occurs, under like circumstances, in a subordinate Lodge. A brother who is disorderly, or contumacious — who refuses to obey the Master, or to conform to the regulations of the Lodge, may be excluded by a vote of the Lodge, or by the direct prerogative of the Master.

It is well to observe here, that the part of the opening ritual which strictly forbids improper conduct, under such penalty as the by-laws prescribe, or a majority of the brethren present see proper to inflict, applies to the state of facts here cited, and not (as many erroneously suppose) to the infliction of the higher grades of punishment because an offence has been committed in view of the Lodge. Temporary exclusion does not deprive a Mason of any of his general relations to the Fraternity, or any of his positive rights (for the right to be in the Lodge is a qualified one, dependent on good behavior,) and hence, when milder remedies—as expostulation or reproof—fail, may be summarily administered to save the credit of the Lodge and preserve its peace and harmony; but when an offence has been committed requiring the infliction of either of the major punishments, then the necessary forms of a trial must be had. This rule is necessary to guard against the effects of sudden passion, which may seize an assembly as effectually as a single individual, and under the influence of which a stigma might be attached to an innocent man that no after repentance could altogether banish. Moreover, if it were in the province of a Lodge to deprive a brother of all his rights in a summary manner, there would be no safety for the minority; for where absolute power

exists, the apology for its exercise is rarely difficult
to find.   Let it be admitted, too, that where a grave
offence has been committed in the very presence of
a Lodge, the result of a formal trial must necessarily
be a foregone conclusion. Still, it is better and more
Masonic to guard against the possibility of error or
misunderstanding by adhering to the forms of trial,
and thus dispensing justice without the semblance of
passion.   It is true that temporary exclusion might
be ordered by the Master without due reflection or
adequate cause, but at the worst the excluded brother would lose nothing but the pleasure of a single
evening in the Lodge, while, on his complaint to the
Grand Master, a more than compensatory justice
might be awarded to the hastily-acting Master or
Lodge.   Not much danger, however, is to be apprehended from this source; for during an active participation of twenty years in the affairs of Masonry,
we have never known of a case. The principle, however, remains the same.

Permanent exclusion was formerly the polite term
for expulsion ; but it is now better known as striking
from the roll—a process by which a brother is summarily deprived of his rights of membership in a
particular Lodge, without trial, and often without
notice.   This practice, which is gradually making its
way among the Grand Lodges, commenced about

the year 1851, and was intended by the authors to afford a milder way of dealing with unwilling or negligent contributors to the Lodge funds than the former one of suspension, it being held that no gen eral deprivation of rights ought to follow mere re missness in paying dues. The remedy has, however, proved many times worse than the original disease ; for a brother stricken from the roll is not only deprived of his membership in his own Lodge, but also of that of affiliating elsewhere, should he be so inclined, because when attempting such affiliation he cannot show an honorable discharge from his first membership, and cannot therefore be admitted to the new one. Striking from the roll is frequently resorted to when it is desired to get rid of an obnoxious member against whom no charges can be found, and he is thus driven into the ranks of the non-affiliated, with a moral certainty that he will remain there. We fully concur in the general sentiment, that no act of suspension should be allowed for nonpayment of dues only, and we think that all the requirements of justice could be answered by excluding from all the rights and benefits of his own Lodge any brother who, after due notice, neglects or refuses to pay his dues (when one year in arrears), conditioned that payment of the amount due at the time of exclusion, if tendered within one year from that

date, should operate his restoration to his former
status without other action; and if more than a year
had elapsed, that then the Lodge, on receiving the
amount due, should grant an honorable discharge;
provided, of course, that no charges are pending.
Lodge dues are a legitimate source of revenue, and
a much better dependence than initiations for the
means to meet current expenses. It is therefore
proper that Lodges should have reasonable power to
enforce payment, but still, one that when used should
not be a worse offence in Masonry than the delinquency against which it is leveled.

Definite Suspension is the first really serious punishment inflicted by Masonic law, because, while in
operation—whether the period be one year or one
day—the suspended brother is deprived of all his
Masonic rights but one, and that is the right to resume his place in the Craft when the suspension expires by its own limitation. If it were otherwise, it
would not be definite, because the Lodge, if required
to act, might refuse a reinstatement, and thus the
suspension would be indefinite. But the name of
the penalty sufficiently determines its character, and
no argument is needed to show that if a brother is
suspended for six months he cannot be suspended
one moment longer without new charges, and a new
trial for some other offence than that just expiated
by the six months' suspension.

Indefinite Suspension is technically considered a higher grade of punishment than where the exact period is specified in the sentence, because in this case a vote of the Lodge is necessary to restoration ; but practically it is less severe, for we incline to the opinion that a motion to take off an indefinite suspension would be in order at any meeting after the promulgation of the sentence. The very terms of the penalty would seem to indicate that by naming no time the Lodge reserved a right to terminate the punishment at pleasure. Beyond this, there is no difference in the two grades. A Mason definitely or indefinitely suspended is—while the penalty operates —deprived of all his rights and privileges as effectually as if he had never been initiated.

Expulsion is the highest penalty known to the Masonic code, and when inflicted absolutely severs all connection between the brother and the Fraternity, for which reason it has been aptly termed Masonic death. This penalty is only inflicted for the most flagrant infractions of moral or Masonic law, and when pronounced by a Lodge is conditional until affirmed by the Grand Lodge, if appeal be taken against it within the time prescribed by the local regulations. If no appeal be taken, no confirmation is needed, because the delinquent may then be said to accept the terms of the sentence. By expulsion, a Mason not only loses his own rights, but his family is thereby deprived of all claim upon the assistance and protection of the Fraternity.

This penalty should only be inflicted after serious deliberation, and when it is believed that the presence of the offender in the Society will produce greater evil than his reformation could be expected to effect good.

A question here arises as to what vote is required to suspend or expel. Reasoning by analogy, we should say that, as in the first Grand Lodge, all questions were decided by a majority vote, so, in the present day, the same general rule ought to apply; but we find a great diversity of opinion existing on this point. Some Grand Lodges require a two-thirds vote; others—New York among the number—a majority. As in various other matters, therefore, the decision will be governed by the regulations of the local Grand Lodge.

Notice of suspension or expulsion is usually sent to the neighboring Lodges, and always to the Grand Secretary; but care must be taken that no publication is made to others than Masons; to avoid which the notices should be in writing.

Lastly, it is now universally admitted that while expulsion or suspension, when inflicted by the authority of symbolic Masonry, debars the brother thus dealt with from all the rights he may have as a Royal Arch Mason or Knight Templar, the same penalties, when inflicted by the higher orders, do not affect his standing in the Lodge, for the reason that the Chapter and Commandery rest upon the Lodge, it being an indispensible prerequisite to admission in them that the candidate shall be in good standing in the preceding degrees; and the same qualification is necessary to maintain membership when acquired. When, therefore, a Knight Templar loses his standing in symbolic Masonry by suspension or expulsion he no longer possesses the requisite qualifications for membership in the Commandery, and can therefore no longer participate in its labors. But the converse of the proposition does not hold good, because, while the Templar is required to have received the degrees of the Lodge and Chapter, and therefore has lawful knowledge of those bodies, the Master Mason knows nothing of the superior grades, and cannot take legal cognizance of their acts; and hence, when the Chapter or Commandery expel one of their members, his standing in his Lodge remains good. If the offence for which he has been expelled in the higher body be one affecting his moral character and standing, the same charge may be brought against him in the Lodge, and he will there be dealt with in the usual way.

SECTION IV.—RESTORATION.

In the Masonic code, restoration is the act of grace, or pardon, extended to the repentant offender after sentence has taken effect, and ought not to be confounded—as it usually is—with reinstatement, when, on appeal, the proceedings in the lower tribunal have been reversed. It is the law that when, after trial and appeal to the Grand Lodge, the sentence has been finally confirmed, and the accused indefinitely suspended or expelled, as the case may be, the Grand Lodge may, on petition, restore the individual to all the general rights and privileges of Masonry, but not to membership in any Lodge; because when the sentence is confirmed by the court of last resort, membership in the Lodge ceases as effectually as if it had never existed, and the reserved right of the Lodge to decide who shall and who shall not be admitted to membership then applies in full force. But, as we have already shown, when on appeal the sentence and proceedings in the first court (the Lodge) are reversed for irregularity or want of proof, then the sentence of suspension or expulsion goes for nothing, because it is declared by the highest authority that it has not been legally pronounced, and therefore not pronounced at all; and, as we have said before, the member continues the standing he enjoyed before the charges were preferred ; which standing had been attacked but not injured by the irregular proceedings. In this case, it is evident that no act of restoration would be performed, because there being no loss of membership there is nothing to restore. It is true that after sentence, and during the proceedings on appeal previous to its final determination, the Lodge would not allow the member to sit or enjoy any of its rights or privileges ; but it will be observed that, while the appeal is pending, the rights of the member are not lost, but only in abeyance, the sentence of the Lodge being always subject to appeal, which appeal would be worse than idle if it left an unjust sentence in effect, or if, when it declared a brother illegally dealt with, it did not by that declaration place him in the exact position occupied by him before the commencement of proceedings.

Definite suspension requires no restoration, because as a brother loses his rights by a sentence for a defined period, so, when that period expires by its own limitation, the cause of the loss ceases, and the effects cease with it.

When a Lodge restores a brother who is under the effects of a final sentence of indefinite suspension or expulsion, it readmits him to membership, because it reverses its own sentence and extends a full pardon for the offence on conviction for which sentence had been pronounced. Restoration by the Grand Lodge is necesarily different, because it may take place without the knowledge or consent of the Lodge, which may still adhere to its original determination. It also frequently happens that a Lodge may be willing that a brother suspended or expelled by it shall be restored to the rights and privileges of a non-affiliated Mason, but not again to his former membership; in which case they allow the restoration to be made by the Grand Lodge, and usually join in the petition for such restoration.

Here again the question occurs : "What vote is necessary to enable a Lodge to restore a brother indefinitely suspended or expelled?" In answer, we can state the general practice, but we cannot give any absolute rule, because there is none. It is commonly held that a two-thirds vote is necessary to restore an indefinitely suspended Mason, but we have never met with any one who could give a valid reason for the requirement beyond the regulations of Grand Lodges. Those bodies restore even from expulsion by a majority vote, and we see no reason why a Lodge may not take off a sentence of indefinite suspension in the same way. Grand Lodge regulations are, however, of greater force than mere opinions, and Lodges must consult and be governed by

them. Restoration from expulsion by a Lodge requires previous proposal and a unanimous vote ; because the sentence of expulsion, when confirmed, is
Masonic death, or, in other words, absolute severance
of all connection between the individual and the Fraternity ; and as the act of restoration puts the individual in possession of full Masonic privileges, it is
necessary that the vote should be unanimous, because the Lodge by restoration admits to membership one who had been severed from it as completely
as if he had never belonged to it, or had voluntarily
dimitted.   Here the distinction between indefinite
suspension and expulsion (which is an extremely nice
one) will be made. A brother who has been suspended, although he is as totally debarred from the
exercise of his Masonic privileges, *for the time being*,
as one expelled, nevertheless retains a *quasi* connection with the Society. "He is not dead, but sleep-
eth." That is, the functions of his Masonic existence
are not absolutely destroyed, but suspended ; and
the removal of this disability would appear to require
a less decided vote than in the case of the major
penalty. It may be added, too, that as this penalty
is inflicted for less serious offences than those requiring expulsion, so, in justice, it ought to require a
less difficult method of restoration than unanimity.

In the act of striking from the roll, it is understood

that the member has forfeited his membership by refusal or neglect to comply with the by-law requiring him to pay annual or quarterly dues, and has, in so doing, violated a contract made by him on his admission as a member. This is a matter belonging to the Lodge—one that does not affect the general relations of the brother to the Fraternity except in depriving him of the power to affiliate elsewhere; and one, consequently, in which reinstatement, and not restoration, is required. If the striking from the roll is performed in accordance with the law of the jurisdiction, then the Grand Lodge cannot interfere to force the member back; but, on the contrary, if there has been irregularity in the proceedings, then, of course, the Grand Lodge, in reversing those proceedings, reinstates the member; because, not having been legally deprived of his rights, he is lawfully entitled to the position he occupied before the illegal act. We hope to see the day when, by general consent, the disabilities arising from mere non-payment of dues may be removed by the payment of the amount of such dues; for as a Mason, while stricken from the roll, cannot enjoy the privileges of the Lodge, neither should he be chargeable with dues during that time.

CHAPTER VIII.

The Grand Lodge.

SECTION I.—THE FORMATION OF GRAND LODGES.

Our readers cannot have failed to observe that we have studiously avoided all reference to authorities of an earlier date than the charges and regulations of 1721, which we consider as sufficient for all the purposes of the present system of Masonic jurisprudence. From this stand-point we feel warranted in making the assertion, that Grand Lodges, as now constituted and conducted, are a modern growth, engrafted on the original stock at the revival of Masonry in 1717, and having no claim whatever to an existence preceding that period. We are aware that the assembly in the city of York, in 926, at which the Gothic constitutions were adopted, and others held at subsequent periods, have been denominated Grand Lodges, but the term is misapplied; they were conventions or general assemblies, having no more similitude to a modern Grand Lodge than a friendly meeting of brethren would resemble the order and regularity that prevail in a formed Lodge. Rebold,

in his " *Histoire General de la Franc-maconnerie*,"
speaks of Grand Lodges (*Haupthutten*) existing in
the fifteenth century, which "had independent and
sovereign jurisdiction, and determined without appeal
all causes brought before them." But they belonged
to the Society of operative Masons or stone-dressers,
to which he and others imagine the present Society
of speculative or Freemasons owes its existence; and
though they may in some degree have been the mod-
els, they certainly had no relation to Grand Lodges
of the present day.

Previous to 1717, an annual assembly and feast
was held at which all the brethren who saw fit were
present, and at which, when required, a Grand Master was elected ; but these meetings fell into decay
until, on the accession of George I., the Masons in
London resolved to cement themselves under a new
Grand Master, and to revive the communications and
annual festivals of the Society. Accordingly, on St.
John the Baptist's day, 1717, in the third year of
the reign of King George I., the assembly and feast
were held, when the oldest Master Mason and the
Master of a Lodge, having taken the chair, a list of
proper candidates for the office of Grand Master was
produced, and the brethren, by a great majority of
hands, elected Mr. Anthony Sayer Grand Master of
Masons for the ensuing year, who was forthwith in-

vested by the oldest Master, installed by the Master of the oldest Lodge, and duly congratulated by the assembly who paid him homage.* This was the beginning of the Grand Lodge of England, from which have sprung the Grand Lodges of the world. At this meeting it was agreed, among other things, " that the privilege of assembling as Masons, which had hitherto been unlimited, should be vested in certain Lodges or assemblies of Masons convened in certain places, and that every Lodge to be hereafter convened, except the four old Lodges at this time existing, should be legally authorized to act by a warrant from the Grand Master for the time being, granted to certain individuals by petition, with the consent and approbation of the Grand Lodge in communication ; and that without such warrant no Lodge should hereafter be deemed regular or constitutional."

Thus was established a central authority or government for the Fraternity, to which was committed the superintendence of the Craft, and entrusted the responsibility of making laws for its observance and for the maintainance of its ancient landmarks; it being also specially agreed " that no law, rule, or regulation, to be thereafter made or passed in the Grand Lodge, should encroach on any landmark which was

* Preston's Illustrations of Masonry—Oliver's edition—p. 150.

11

at that time established as the standard of Masonic government."[*]

The Grand Lodge thus inaugurated underwent, within a brief period, various modifications. Many new Lodges being formed, it was soon found that a general attendance of the brethren would make the body too unwieldy, and the present system of representation by the Masters and Wardens was established. The right to confer the three degrees was ceded to the Lodges, and the Grand Lodge then became what it is now—the supreme tribunal and legislature of the Craft within its jurisdiction.

The first Grand Lodge, it will be observed, was established by the concurrent action of the brethren of the four old Lodges, acting as individuals, as is evident from the fact stated by Preston, that when matters had been adjusted to the satisfaction of the brethren of the four old Lodges, they considered their attendance on the future communications of the society as unnecessary ; and, like the other Lodges, trusted implicitly to their Masters and Wardens, resting satisfied that no measure of importance would be adopted without their approbation. It is now held that no Grand Lodge can be established without the concurrence of three or more regular Lodges previously established, and acting through their Masters and Wardens. We shall refer to this again

* PRESTON.

when we come to speak of the jurisdictional rights of Grand Lodges.

SECTION II.—THE POWERS OF GRAND LODGES.

A Grand Lodge is now defined to be "a body of Masons in whom is inalienably vested the government and superintendence of the Fraternity within its territorial jurisdiction, and is primarily composed of its Grand officers and the Masters and Wardens, or their proxies, of the several subordinate Lodges under its jurisdiction."[*]   It is necessarily supreme in the exercise of all powers not specially reserved to the Lodges, and there is of course no appeal from its decisions ; but it cannot make or pass any regulation in derogation of the Ancient Landmarks.

The powers of a Grand Lodge are : Legislative, Judicial, and Executive, which are exercised under the limitations above specified, but which are inoperative beyond the political limits of the country, State, or territory in which it may be located, and from which it usually derives its name—as the Grand Lodge of England, of New York, etc.

The Legislative powers of a Grand Lodge extend to all matters relating to the Craft save those inherent in, and reserved to, the Lodges.   The laws made by it have general effect throughout the bounds of its

---

[*] Constitution G. L. of N. Y.

jurisdiction, and its decisions are final and without appeal; though it may, like all other legislative bodies, revise its own proceedings, and alter, amend, or annul them, as set forth in the thirty-ninth of the General Regulations. In the exercise of this power, a Grand Lodge may enact a constitution and regulations for its own government and for the government of the Fraternity which it represents, and may alter or amend that instrument in accordance with its own provisions. It may levy a tax on its subordinates, or require the payment of a certain portion of their revenues into its treasury, for the purpose of defraying its necessary expenses. It may grant warrants constituting new Lodges, by which they become components of the great Masonic family, and enact laws for their better regulation and convenience. It may establish and preserve a uniform mode of work and lectures, under sanction of the Ancient Landmarks and usages of Masonry. It may hear, and entertain or reject, all appeals, memorials, petitions, or resolutions that may be presented in proper form.

The Legislative power of the Grand Lodge is the one which, from its nature and the habits of our people, is, in this country, most likely to be abused; nay, the one that is already responsible for much evil. The tendency to over-legislate, common to all deliberative bodies, is becoming more apparent every year ; and conservative men already foresee troubles arising in the future from this source. Nor can it be doubted, that the original intention of the founders of the Grand Lodge system—the objects they sought to attain by yielding a portion of their rights —have been, and are constantly being, overstepped ; that the reserved rights of the Lodges are being gradually encroached upon, and the powers of the Grand Lodge correspondingly increased. The result may be easily divined, and will manifest itself— as it has already done in some instances—in the assertion of a claim to sole and supreme authority in all matters relating to the Craft. It is the duty of the brethren at large to counteract this evil tendency, and maintain their reserved rights intact by a more careful scrutiny of Grand Lodge doings, and by instructing their representatives so that they shall, when in Grand Lodge, represent their constituents rather than themselves. There is also a minor evil growing out of excessive legislation which is simply annoying to the brethren, without producing any benefit to the institution. We refer to the mania for making laws and regulations on every conceivable topic, nine-tenths of which ought reasonably to be left to the discretion of Lodges, and the interference with which tends to exasperate them, and sets their wits at work to discover some means by which the rule may be evaded.

As a matter of right, the legislation of a Grand Lodge ought always to be prospective in its action ; retroactive, or *ex post facto*, laws being regarded in all communities as unjust, oppressive and destructive of the rights of communities and individuals.

The Judicial powers of a Grand Lodge are of two kinds : original and appellate. Original judicial power is exercised by the Grand Lodge in the trial of charges against any of its officers for malfeasance in office, except the Grand Master ; in the settlement of controversies between Lodges, or between individual members of different Lodges, or in the trial of a Master of a Lodge against whom charges are preferred. It also may assume original jurisdiction in cases which come before it on appeal, by increasing the penalty awarded by the original court. It also exercises original jurisdiction in the forfeiture or revocation of warrants, which generally results from evil practices on the part of the Lodge, which is therefor put on trial. As one Lodge cannot entertain charges against another, and proceed to try them, it necessarily follows that the Grand Lodge, being the common superior, is the appropriate tribunal for the trial of such cases. Warrants thus forfeited may of course be returned by the Grand Lodge at its pleasure. The judicial powers of the Grand Lodge are, however, most frequently exercised in the decision of appeals from the individual members of the Fraternity against the action of their Lodges, or the decisions of their Masters, and its decisions are final and binding on the parties, because there being no Masonic authority superior to the Grand Lodge, it is the court of last resort.

The Executive powers of a Grand Lodge are those in the exercise of which it administers the laws and enforces the decisions made by it in its legislative and judicial capacity. And whatever may have been the practice in former days, it is now certain that they are exercised for no other purpose. While, however, a Grand Lodge, when in session, confines its action to the administration of the laws it has enacted, there can be no doubt that it may extend the sphere of its action, by a change of its constitution, to all matters not in absolute derogation of the inherent rights of Lodges. Thus, if there were no constitutional impediment, it might initiate, pass, and raise a profane, because it is the authority from whence the subordinates derive their right to make Masons ; but it could not make the brother it raised a member of any Lodge, for that is an inherent prerogative of the Lodges themselves, with which the Grand Lodge cannot interfere.

The executive power of a Grand Lodge is, however, in a great degree entrusted to the Grand Mas-

ter, and by him exercised during the recess—a necessity arising from the fact that the Grand Lodges
of the United States, with perhaps two or three exceptions, having by common consent abolished Quarterly Communications, meet annually only. These
meetings seldom last more than three or four days;
so that for three hundred and sixty days in the year
the administration and execution of the laws is entrusted to the Grand Master; and the probability is
that, all things considered, the laws are more carefully executed by him than they would or could be
by the Grand Lodge.

The Jurisdictional rights of a Grand Lodge do not
extend beyond the bounderies of the country, State,
or territory where it is located, except where a country is Masonically vacant; that is, having no Grand
Lodge established in it; in which case all the Grand
Lodges in the world have concurrent jurisdiction
there, so far as they may deem it proper to be exercised; so that in a vacant territory one or a dozen
Grand Lodges may charter subordinates, and each
would be equally justified in so doing. When, however, a majority of the subordinates (being not less
than three in number) choose to establish a Grand
Lodge, then the territory is occupied; and not only
are Grand Lodges in other States or countries forbidden to exercise any powers in the territory occu-

pied by the new Grand Lodge, but their subordinates (if any) that may have refused to unite in the formation of the Grand Lodge, are to be withdrawn or left subject to the disposition of the local authority."* It is the assertion of this doctrine that has been, and still is, the cause of difficulty between the Grand Lodges of New York and Hamburgh. The latter body, not content with superintending the affairs of its own jurisdiction, has thought proper to create new Lodges owing fealty and obedience to it, but located in the State of New York, and therefore within the bounds of the lawful Grand Lodge of that State. The Grand Lodge of New York very properly objects to this invasion of its territory, because : 1st. It was the first to occupy the jurisdiction now occu-

---

* A case in point occurred in the Grand Encampment of the United States, in 1859. That body had established subordinates in the State of Michigan to the number of four. Three of these subordinates united in forming a State Grand Commandery, but one refused to do so, and claimed the right to continue its allegiance to the Grand Éncampment of the U. S. The Committee on Jurisprudence reported : "That in all the branches of Masonry in this country the law obtains that a State Grand Body has sole and exclusive jurisdiction within the limits of the territory it occupies. There can be no divided jurisdiction, nor can any authority give legal existence to a subordinate in contravention of the will of the State Superior." Whereupon it was resolved : "That the Grand Commandery of Michigan, from the date of its formation, has of right exercised sole and exclusive jurisdiction over all subordinates in that State."

pied by it — its existence antedating the political formation of the State. 2d. That occupation has been continuous to the present moment; and 3d. Because the Grand Lodges of the world, Hamburgh excepted, agree that every Grand Lodge has sole and exclusive jurisdiction within the limits of the territory in which it is located; and hence, that no Grand Lodge has the shadow of a right to plant Lodges in the territory of its neighbor without its consent. If, therefore, the difficulty is ever adjusted, it must be by the Grand Lodge of Hamburgh retiring from its unjustifiable and unfraternal violation of an universal law.

We have already spoken of Lodge jurisdiction in its appropriate place. That jurisdiction is restrained or extended by Grand Lodges, especially in the modern rule forbidding the initiation of non-residents. Having already given the reasons for its adoption, it is only necessary to say that although accepted as a law by the Grand Lodges of the United States, it is not generally so in Europe. The probability is, however, that in the progress of time it will become universal.

CHAPTER IX.

The Grand Officers.

IN all Grand Lodges and Grand Orients there is a Grand Master, but the remaining officers vary in title, number and prerogative according to the customs of the country, the rite practiced, or the supposed necessities of the Grand Body itself. Thus, in England there is a Deputy Grand Master and Provincial Grand Masters appointed by the Grand Master, and in some cases a "Pro. Grand Master, who can only be appointed when the Masonic throne is occupied by a prince of the blood royal. And to be qualified for the situation it is requisite that his worldly rank be commensurate with the dignity of the office and the representative of royalty. He must, therefore, be a peer of the realm, as well as the Past Master of a Lodge. His collar and jewel, like his authority, must be precisely the same as that of the Grand Master; and in case of a vacancy, he actually assumes the office until the next annual election."[*] In France there is no Deputy Grand Master, but in his place several assistant or acting Grand Masters, who form the council of the Grand Master, dispose of the routine business of the Grand Orient, and preside at

[*] OLIVER.

its meetings in the absence of the chief officer. In the United States, where all the Grand Lodges profess to be of the so-called "Ancient York Rite," the officers are :

A Grand Master (whose style is Most Worshipful).

A Deputy Grand Master.

A Senior Grand Warden.

A Junior Grand Warden.

A Grand Treasurer.

A Grand Secretary.

A Grand Chaplain.

A Grand Marshal.

A Grand Standard Bearer.

A Grand Sword Bearer.

Two or more Grand Stewards.

A Senior Grand Deacon.

A Junior Grand Deacon.

(All of whom are styled Right Worshipful.)

A Grand Pursuivant.

A Grand Tyler.

(Who are styled Worshipful.)

In some Grand Lodges there is a Grand Orator, a Grand Lecturer, and District Deputy Grand Masters, and in others no Grand Pursuivant. In Pennsylvania the Grand Master is styled Right Worshipful, and the remaining officers Worshipful. These variations are of no particular importance other than affording proof of an unfortunate tendency to lose sight of that uniformity which ought to characterize our institution in all its doings, and to which, we apprehend, our successors will wish we had paid more attention.

Let us now examine the powers and duties of the several Grand officers above enumerated.

THE GRAND MASTER.

Like the King, in monarchical countries, the Grand Master never dies. That is to say, the office, its powers and prerogatives, remain intact whatever may become of the individual who, for the time being, is their custodian ; and hence, the acts of a Grand Master survive his tenure of office, and pass to his successor, to be by him maintained or reversed as circumstances may to him appear to require.

The office of Grand Master has always existed. In all the history and traditions of the Craft, we can find no time when the Fraternity was not governed by a chief officer styled a Grand Master. His office is, therefore, not a creation of the Ancient Charges and regulations, nor of any modern constitution. And yet, while his prerogatives are in some things beyond any control but that of the Landmarks, it is not in all, from the fact that since the formation of Grand Lodges, the government of those bodies and of the

Fraternity owing them allegiance is founded on written constitutions, which the Grand Master, in common with the humblest Mason under his jurisdiction,
is bound to observe and respect. Indeed, he enters
into a solemn engagement at his installation, that he
will do so, and he therefore waives, to that extent,
his unlimited prerogatives. It will be found, moreover, that the commonly received notion that there
can be no appeal from the decision of the Grand
Master is not strictly true ; for on examining the
transactions of Grand Lodges, it will be seen that
the judgment of the Grand Master is overruled, and
that to do otherwise would be, in fact, to admit his
entire freedom from the weakness of human nature
—a proposition too absurd for argument. The sovereignty, as we have repeatedly said, is in the Craft
at large, and by their delegation is exercised by the
Grand Lodge as their agent ; and the final decision
of a case by that body, in annual communication, is
in reality the only one from which there is no appeal.
It is true, that during the interval from one session
of the Grand Lodge to another, its executive powers
are vested in the Grand Master, and all the high prerogatives of his office are then in full force ; but they
are exercised by him on the condition of a review by
the Grand Lodge, whenever a majority of its members think proper to exercise that right. This re-

served power of the Grand Lodge is distinctly seen in the nineteenth article of the Regulations of 1721. "If the Grand Master should abuse his power, and render himself unworthy of the obedience and subjection of the Lodges, he shall be treated in a way and manner to be agreed upon in a new regulation; because hitherto the ancient Fraternity have had no occasion for it, their former Grand Masters having all behaved themselves worthy of that honorable office." Here we observe the distinct assertion of a power to exercise discipline over the Grand Master, in any way that may be agreed upon in a new regulation, and that if the power has not been exercised, it is because the brethren chosen to the responsible station of Grand Master have so demeaned themselves as not to require it. But of the right there can be no question. Now, if the Grand Master can be put on trial, he can—the proof warranting—be expelled from the rights and privileges of the Craft; and it follows that the same power that may discipline him, may also exercise the lesser act of sovereignty in reversing his decisions. We may be accused of taking an extreme view, and dispelling certain illusions that have hitherto been maintained, but we disclaim any such intention, and seek only to bring about a proper understanding of the real powers of the officer of whom we are treating. We should be the last to lower the popular reverence for our chief officer, but we deem it well that his true position should be understood, both for the sake of the officer himself and for that of the Craft under his authority. Whatever, therefore, may have been the original powers of the Grand Master, there can be no doubt but that those powers are now in some things amenable to the provisions of Grand Lodge constitutions and legislation, and that every Grand Master accepts office with a proviso that he will not only enforce the laws and execute the legislative acts of the Grand Lodge, but that he will do so under the sanction of those laws and acts; or, in other words, that while he exacts obedience from others, he will furnish a proper example by himself obeying the laws he executes.

There are, of course, some of the powers belonging to the Grand Master which are in themselves landmarks, and therefore not subject to legislation; but even these have yielded to the force of public opinion, as will be seen in the following enumeration of the prerogatives of the Grand Master.

1. To convene the Grand Lodge at any time he may in his discretion deem proper. This is precisely the same power exercised by a Master of a Lodge, and is subject to the same restriction; namely, that the meetings thus called are but special or

emergent meetings, at which no business affecting the general interests of the Craft can be transacted. The stated meeting of the Grand Lodge is its Annual Communication, which meeting is always provided for in the constitution or regulations, and is therefore not subject to the call of the Grand Master, nor has he any power to change it; for if he had such power, and should exercise it, then the meeting would not be the Annual Communication, and the usual business of that session could not be lawfully transacted. At the Annual Communication, too, the order of business is generally fixed by regulation, which the Grand Master cannot change of his own authority, because he has agreed to observe and enforce the regulations of the Grand Lodge.

2. To preside at all meetings of the Grand Lodge, whether stated or special. Although installed and proclaimed the Grand Master of Masons, his relations to the Grand Lodge are the same in this respect as those of a Master to his Lodge. He is therefore, by virtue of his office, the presiding officer, and it is the law that while so presiding there can be no appeal from his decision to that of the Grand Lodge —a law which, though generally observed, has its exceptions; usually effected, it is true, by indirection, but effected none the less.

3. To summon any Lodge in the jurisdiction, to

preside therein, and to require an account of its doings. This is one of the undoubted prerogatives of
the Grand Master—one that is free from any restraint
but his own judgment, and one that is in keeping
with the nature of his office and the general principles of the society, which make him the overseer of
the Craft and necessarily clothe him with all the
power requisite to an efficient discharge of such important duties.

4. To grant his letters of dispensation for the
formation of new Lodges under such restrictions as
may be provided in the constitution of his Grand
Lodge. As, for instance, it is provided in the constitution of the Grand Lodge of New York, "that no
dispensation to form a new Lodge shall be issued
within three months of the Annual Communication,"
that a certain fee shall be exacted, and that certain
recommendations should accompany the petition.
Now, it is true that the Grand Master might disre-
gard all these requirements and issue his dispensation to form a new Lodge, which would have to be
respected till the next Annual Communication of the
Grand Lodge ; but it is clear that the body would
not sanction so palpable a violation of its statutes,
even at the hands of the Grand Master—that hence
it would refuse to recognize the new Lodge or its
work, and therefore the Grand Master is bound, as

an act of justice to the petitioners and in view of his
own covenants, to respect the regulations that are
made by his Grand Lodge. The Grand Master of
England grants a full warrant, but the sanction of
the Grand Lodge is required to complete the standing of the Lodge, so that in reality there is but the
difference of a name between the acts of the English
Grand Master in constituting a new Lodge and that
of an American Grand Master in issuing his dispensation to effect the same purpose. The real
exercise of power in this respect being the right
vested in the Grand Master to withhold his dispensation ; in which case it would, as a general thing,
be folly on the part of the petitioners to expect a
warrant from the Grand Lodge. Dispensations are
likewise granted by the Grand Master for various
purposes ; as—to shorten the interval between the
degrees, for processions, and other purposes ; but
generally, if not always, in accordance with the requirements of the general regulations of the Grand
Lodge.

5. To constitute new Lodges and instal their officers when a warrant has been issued by the Grand
Lodge. · This appears to be an independent power,
for it is conceded that the warrant is of no effect until the Lodge has been duly constituted and its officers installed—the power to do which is vested in

the Grand Master, and can only be exercised by him
or by his duly appointed agent or proxy. So, too, in
the laying of corner-stones and the dedication of Masonic halls, the Grand Master acts by the inherent
authority of his office.

6. To arrest the charter of a Lodge, or to suspend
the Master or any of the officers from the functions
of their respective stations until the annual meeting
of the Grand Lodge. Under the constitution of the
Grand Lodge of New York the Grand Master may
absolutely suspend a warrant, and with it, in his discretion, all the members of the Lodge ; but this is
an exceptional case, the general rule being that the
Grand Master simply arrests the powers of the warrant for the time being, without in any way affecting
the validity of that instrument ; that is, he forbids
any further meetings of the Lodge, or the transaction of any business by it, until the next Annual Communication of the Grand Lodge ; but if at that annual meeting the Grand Lodge should fail to take
action, the warrant would instantly become valid,
and all the lawful powers accruing under it would at
once inure to the Lodge, as completely as if no arrest had taken place. This prerogative is therefore
but a part of the executive or supervisory power
vested in the Grand Master during the recess of the
Grand Lodge, and is exercised by him as the agent

of the body and subject to such action as may appear judicious to it, when the facts are presented in the annual report of the officer. The recall of a Lodge under dispensation would of course be a finality, because the process of creating a Lodge not having been completed by the vote of the Grand Lodge authorizing a warrant of constitution to issue, the Lodge would not have taken its place in the great family, nor would it be entitled to the immunities and privileges belonging to a regularly warranted and duly constituted Lodge.

7. The right to make Masons at sight. This is undoubtedly an inherent and inalienable prerogative of the Grand Master, accorded to him by the Ancient Landmarks, and therefore not to be affected by any legislation of the Grand Lodge, except in so far as he may be willing to be advised by the lawfully expressed will of the brethren,"* but is one which is seldom exercised, and one that will gradually become a tradition by the growing force of opinion, which is rapidly being educated into a belief that there should be but one entrance to the fold and that all aspirants should pass through it in like manner and under

---

* Thus, in 1861, a resolution was passed by the Grand Lodge of New York, requesting the Grand Master not to issue dispensations to authorize the conferring three degrees on a candidate at one meeting (which is in reality making Masons at sight), since which time no such dispensation has been issued.

similar restrictions. This prerogative has been the
subject of a vast amount of discussion within a few
years past, the net result of which seems to be a
general concurrence in the opinion that the Grand
Master may make Masons at sight, but that he must
do so in a regular Lodge. The proviso, however,
amounts to nothing, for the Grand Master certainly
has power to do in person what he can authorize
others to do by his dispensation, and as no one will
dispute the right of a Lodge U. D. to make Masons,
it follows that any six Master Masons summoned by
the Grand Master to assist him, would, with himself,
be to all intents and purposes a regular Lodge, convened at the will of the Grand Master and dissolved
by a stroke of his gavel, when the purpose of its
meeting had been accomplished. The restriction is
therefore but an indication of the general sentiment,
that Masons ought not to be made at all, except in
the way provided in the old regulations ; that is, by
previous notice, due inquiry, and after unanimous
acceptance by some regular Lodge, at a stated communication. It has been well said by the M. W.
John L. Lewis : "There is no conceivable case which,
to my mind, presents a *necessity* for the exercise of
the power. It ever resolves itself into a question of
convenience. Going upon a voyage or a long journey
leads to the inquiry why the petition was not made

in a proper time before the voyage or journey was undertaken. If a return be contemplated, then the petition can await the return. The dispensing power which arrests the requirements of written constitutions, nay, of landmarks, cannot be a landmark itself, and should be exercised with caution. Every candidate should pass the investigations of a discreet committee and the scrutiny of a secret ballot, before admission to the portals of our Temple. "Making Masons at sight" leads to hasty and imperfect work —to half-comprehended and confusedly-received instruction, and frequently to differences among brethren. It is the fruitful source of complaint where these hastily-made Masons go. The exercise of the power is asked always from selfish, not to say mercenary motives; for the avowed object is always some personal advantage to the applicant. It rarely benefits the candidate who thus receives the degrees, and its refusal can rarely injure him. The rush at the gates of the institution is sufficiently great without the action of Grand officers to smooth the way." Few Masons having the good of the Craft at heart will dispute the truth of the words here quoted; and it is to be hoped that the day is not far distant when, by common consent, making Masons at sight will be among the things heard of but not seen.

8. The power to heal irregularly-made Masons.

Having occasion, a few years since, to investigate this topic in an official capacity, we found two questions presenting themselves for solution. First— What is healing? and secondly, By what authority is it to be performed? We found great diversity of opinion among those we had always looked to for authority, and, after much correspondence and discussion, finally arrived at the conclusion that to heal is in reality to remake the irregular Mason—abbreviating the ceremonies, omitting the monitorial instruction, but giving the essentials as in the case of a profane. As this process is equivalent to making Masons at sight, it readily follows that the power to control it is in the Grand Master, and that he may exercise it in person or by dispensation to any regular Lodge in his jurisdiction.

9. The right of appointment. By referring to the regulations of 1721, it will be seen that originally the Grand Master wielded an almost unlimited patronage, in the way of appointments to the subordinate offices of the Grand Lodge. He named his Deputy and Wardens and various other officers required, except the Treasurer, who was always elected. In England and on the continent such is the custom to this day, but in the United States the first six officers of a Grand Lodge are generally made elective, while the remainder are usually appointed by the

Grand Master. He likewise appoints the committees and representatives near other Grand Lodges and Grand Orients.

10. As a necessary adjunct of the appointing power there can be no doubt but that the Grand Master may, in the exercise of his discretion, summon any Grand officer before him, require an account of his doings, and for cause suspend him from the functions of his office, or even remove him altogether.

11. By the constitutions of 1721 the Grand Master is entitled to two votes, but this is understood to apply only to cases of a tie, when he gives the casting vote.

It will be seen from the foregoing summary that the powers of the Grand Master are not as absolute as the popular traditions would have us believe—that even the powers which are indisputably his are seldom exercised but in obedience to the regulations established by the Grand Lodge, and that as he is the first Mason in his jurisdiction, so he should be the most prompt in his obedience to the laws which he administers. Of the powers of the Grand Master, Dr. Oliver well says : " There are instances in which it is presumed that the Grand Master can do no wrong, because he is protected by his prerogative and justified by an appeal to the Grand Lodge. But this is a doubtful doctrine, and ought to be received

12

with caution, although it derives a negative corroboration from the constitution of 1721, which admits that an abuse of power has never yet occurred, and therefore it is unprovided for by the text of Masonic law."

" The Grand Lodges of the United States entertain adverse opinions on this point ; for while those of Maryland and Florida have pronounced that an 'appeal from the decision of the Grand Master is an anomaly at war with every principle of Freemasonry, and as such not for a moment to be tolerated or countenanced,' others have promulgated a contrary doctrine ; but even these admit that the only real and practical penalty at their disposal is the free expression of public opinion on his presumed delinquencies. But as the power of the Grand Master is derived from the Grand Lodge, and that body is composed of delegates elected by the private Lodges, if he should commit any flagrant act of injustice the veto of the latter will determine, at the ensuing election, whether he shall continue in an office whose license he has abused by ignoring the opinions of the Craft and acting in open violation of the constitutions. For what is each private Lodge but a local legislature, while the Grand Lodge constitutes a vent for the collective wisdom of its members."

" It is well for the general interests of Masonry

that such is the fact; for it is a sound doctrine that the opinions of the whole united body ought to sway the counsels of their delegates, and prevent any offensive exercise of arbitrary power in the Grand Master."

"Prejudice, partiality, or caprice, may influence the judgment of a single individual, and produce deplorable consequences, however virtuous in intention or honorable in conduct he may be, which in deliberative bodies of men could never happen. Such is the security which Masons possess against the wilful aggression of their rulers."

The Grand Master is required by the ancient regulations, and all subsequent constitutions, to be elected annually, but it does not follow that there need necessarily to be a change at each election. The tendency is indeed the other way—especially in Europe, where it may almost be said to be a life tenure. "During the last century," says Dr. Oliver, "the prevailing custom was to change the Grand Master every year or two, in order to induce a greater number of the nobility to enter the Order, who were by this practice furnished with an opportunity of being placed at its head, and acquiring for the remainder of their lives the distinguished rank of a Past Grand Master; but for the last sixty or seventy years the office has been a life appointment. His

Royal Highness the Duke of Cambridge was elected in 1781, and held the office nine years. At his death, in 1790, His Royal Highness the Prince of Wales was elected in his stead. He held the office twenty-three years, and when he became Prince Regent, in 1813, he resigned the Grand Mastership and assumed the title of Grand Patron, and his brother, the Duke of Sussex, was elected, who held the office till his death, in 1843, being thirty years. The present Grand Master was then chosen, and has filled the throne ever since." So that at present England has no Past Grand Master. Instances are not wanting, in our own country, of long tenure of office, as in the case of the late M. W. Philip C. Tucker, of Vermont, and others; but our bustling, active life, and the fact that our Grand Masters are usually business men, make the political axiom of "rotation in office" apply till it has become a rule sanctioned by custom to consider two years as about the term of service that may be required of one incumbent. The present Grand Master of France, Marshall Magnan, was appointed to his station by the Emperor, without the formality of an election by the representatives of the Fraternity in the Grand Orient. This proceeding was evidently a political *coup*, as the French term it, and was doubtless acquiesced in by the Craft to prevent worse consequences befalling them. A subsequent attempt to coerce the society into the adoption of measures that would have made it a mere puppet in the hands of the astute monarch, was, however, gallantly and successfully resisted, showing that there, as elsewhere, the brethren are not disposed to yield up the inherent sovereignty that of right belongs to them.

THE DEPUTY GRAND MASTER.

Unlike the office of Grand Master, which has always existed, that of Deputy is a creation of the Regulations of 1721, previous to which time there does not appear to have been such an officer. As the title indicates, he is the immediate assistant of the Grand Master, and his lawful successor when from any cause the Grand Master is unable to act. The object of his appointment may be gathered from the sixteenth article of the Regulations of 1721 : "The Grand Master should receive no intimation of business concerning Masonry, but from his Deputy first, except in such certain cases as his Worship can well judge of ; for if the application to the Grand Master be irregular, he can easily order the Grand Wardens, or any other brethren thus applying, to wait upon his Deputy, who is to prepare the business speedily, and lay it orderly before his Worship."

He has no powers but such as are specially conferred upon him by his Grand Lodge constitution, and as these vary somewhat in each jurisdiction, it would be difficult, if not impossible, to state any general rule applying to his office. In the State of New York, the Deputy Grand Master is clothed with considerable power; he may grant dispensations to create new Lodges and for conferring degrees, arrest charters, etc., but as all his acts are liable to be reversed at any time by the Grand Master, he necessarily proceeds with great caution. In Minnesota, his powers are altogether latent, and only to be called into exercise in case of the death, absence, or inability of the Grand Master. Thus, a dispensation to form a new Lodge, granted by the Deputy in that State, was held to be irregular, and the Masons made under it were required to be healed. We incline to the opinion that Minnesota is right, and that the true office of the Deputy Grand Master is to prepare any business concerning Masonry that may be required to be laid before the Grand Master, to act as his proxy when required, and be prepared in case of need to succeed to his functions. In the United States, the Deputy Grand Master is generally elected, but in other countries he is appointed by the Grand Master.

THE GRAND WARDENS.

The duties of a Grand Warden are similar to those of the Warden of a particular Lodge. They stand next in rank and dignity to the Deputy Grand Master, and succeed in order of seniority to the duties of the Grand Master when required so to do by the absence of their superior officers. As in the Lodge, too, the offices of Senior and Junior Grand Warden are entirely separate, and it does not follow that because the Senior Grand Warden is absent, that the Junior is to take his place, or that in the absence of the Deputy the Senior Grand Warden is to sit on the left of the Grand Master, but in case of a vacancy in either office it is to be temporarily filled by appointment of the Grand Master. The rule of succession only applies, in either case, when all the superior officers are absent. They have no other prerogative except that of presiding in subordinate Lodges whenever they are present in company with the Grand Master. They form part of the cabinet or council of the Grand Master, and are always consulted in relation to the business of the Grand Lodge. In Europe, they are appointed. In this country, the Grand Lodges reserve the right of electing them.

THE GRAND TREASURER.

The duties of this officer are strictly financial. He takes charge of all the properties, funds, and vouchers of the Grand Lodge, pays all orders properly drawn upon the money in his custody, is required to give bonds for the faithful performance of his duties, to submit his books and vouchers to inspection whenever required by the Grand Master or Grand Lodge, and to pay over to his successor all funds, property, and vouchers remaining in his hands at the expiration of his term of office.

The first Grand Treasurer seems to have been appointed in 1727, and the duties expected of him are very fully defined in the old Regulations. He continued in office till 1738, when a Grand Treasurer was elected, and since that time the office has always been filled by the votes of the members of the Grand Lodge. He is by virtue of his office a member of the body.

GRAND SECRETARY.

This office was first created in 1723, and has grown in importance with the vast proportions assumed by the society till now it is at once a post of distinction and a laborious charge upon its incumbent. Its duties are of such a responsible nature that none but men of education and refinement should accept its honors, or be elected to the discharge of its duties. As the amanuensis of the Grand Lodge, the Grand Secretary is brought into contact with brethren from all parts of the globe, and should be able by his urbanity and courtesy to convey a favorable impression of the body he represents. He not only issues summons for all meetings of the Grand Lodge and its committees, but is bound to attend them with his books when required, in order that he may impart information and take a careful record of the proceedings, to be read for information at subsequent meetings and to be preserved in the archives for future reference. The returns of all subordinate Lodges are made to him, and he is in most jurisdictions required to keep a correct registry of their members. He is to receive, duly file, and safely keep all papers and documents of the Grand Lodge, to sign and certify all instruments emanating from it, to receive and keep a proper account of all moneys of the Grand Lodge and pay them over to the Grand Treasurer, and to report annually to his Grand Lodge a detailed account of his acts. In addition to his clerical duties, he is frequently—in this country—the chairman of the Committee on Foreign Correspondence, and is charged with the correspondence of the Grand Lodge, under direction of the Grand Master. In the important and often delicate questions that are treated in this correspondence, great tact and discrimination are required, and the mental calibre of the officer is here put to its severest test. Though but limited discretion is given the Grand Secretary in recording the official transactions of the Grand Lodge, which, being presented in the form of written resolutions, reports, etc., he has little more to do than to arrange in the order of their presentation, he may, and ought, by a proper use of the material that passes through his hands, prepare and preserve a history of the great Masonic events of his day that should have the quality of correctness and the value of being official.

This office comes nearest a life-tenure of any connected with our Grand Lodges, the same brother being generally continued in it by successive re-elections as long as he chooses to serve.

THE GRAND CHAPLAINS.

This office, although of modern origin, the first Grand Chaplain having been appointed in 1775, has now very properly been assigned a place in' all the American Grand Lodges. It is a graceful tribute to that religious principle that should underlie all great institutions, and is peculiarly becoming in our Grand Lodges, which admit the fundamental truths all religions, but pay no heed to the distinctions of creed or sect, it being no uncommon thing for several Grand Chaplains to be appointed, each of whom represents a different religious denomination. The duty of a Grand Chaplain is to conduct the religious ceremonies of the Grand Lodge, as well in its usual assemblies as on occasions of public ceremony.

THE GRAND MARSHAL.

This is an office which seems to have been created in the days when Masonic processions were more frequent than they are now, or, we trust, are ever likely to become again, and the duty of this officer— as the name implies—was to conduct them. In these days, and in such Grand Lodges as appoint a Grand Marshal, he is stationed near the Grand Master, to assist in maintaining order and observing such commands as may be given him by the presiding officer. He is required to take charge of processions of the Grand Lodge, should any occur.

THE GRAND STANDARD BEARER.

This is one of the appointed officers in some Grand Lodges, but by no means in all. His duty is to take charge of the banner of the Grand Lodge in all public processions.

THE GRAND SWORD BEARER.

Like the Standard Bearer, this officer is appointed by the Grand Master. His special duty is to carry the state sword immediately in front of the Grand Master, in public ceremonials in which the Grand Lodge participates.

THE GRAND STEWARDS.

These officers, as implied by their title, were formerly charged, in conjunction with the Grand Wardens, with the preparations for the annual feast, an indispensible accompaniment of the Grand Annual Communication which was held on St. John's Day, in June or December, as the Grand Lodge by regulation should decide—usually in June. They made the necessary purchases, sold the tickets bearing the Grand Master's seal, and rendered their accounts to the Grand Lodge " after dinner," as will be found in the thirteenth and fourteenth of the old Regulations. Such, we believe, is the custom in England to this day ; but in America the annual feast—except, perhaps, in one or two instances—has become obsolete, and the communications of Grand Lodges are devoted to the regular business of the Craft. The Grand Stewards are now generally charged with the investigation of applications for assistance on the part of indigent brethren, widows, and orphans, from the funds of the Grand Lodge.

THE GRAND DEACONS

Are appointed officers, and like the Deacons of a Lodge are the messengers of the Grand Master and Grand Wardens. They are stationed near the Grand Master, in all public processions and ceremonials. The Grand Marshal, Grand Standard Bearer, Grand Sword Bearer, Grand Stewards, and Grand Deacons have no powers or prerogatives, merely obeying such orders as may be issued to them, and are generally termed, in military parlance, the Staff of the Grand Master.

THE GRAND POURSUIVANT,

Whose title comes down to us from the days of chivalry, is a kind of assistant Tyler, and exercises functions analagous to those of the Junior Deacon of a Lodge, being placed inside the porch of the Temple to maintain order among those congregated there, and to see that none pass or repass without the requisite permission.

THE GRAND TYLER,

Like his prototype in the subordinate Lodge, is placed outside the gate and charged with watch and

ward against all who are not entitled to pass. **Al-**
though the lowest in rank **of** the Grand officers, he
is certainly **not the** least important, **for** on him rests
the responsibility of **a** careful guard against cowans
and a courteous welcome to the true. It is of the
highest importance that he should not lightly vouch
for any one ; for, as having been present with a per-
son in Grand Lodge is considered the highest au-
thority for admitting him to **a** subordinate one, a
mistake here might lead to many others. The Grand
Poursuivant and Grand Tyler are usually **Past Mas-**
ters of long standing, and are generally paid a moderate salary for their services.

THE GRAND LECTURER.

In the earlier days of Masonry on the American
continent, it was usual to appoint a number of brethren in each Grand Lodge jurisdiction, under the title
of "Grand Visitors," who were employed in journey-
ing about the State, visiting the Lodges, examining
their work, instructing them when required, and attending to such other business connected with the
welfare of the Craft as might be confided to them by
the Grand Lodge or Grand Master; but with the increase of Lodges and Masons, the labor has been
divided, the "work" being placed in charge of Grand
Lecturers, and the other business in that of District

Deputy Grand Masters. The present idea of a Grand Lecturer seems to be, that he shall have the quality of being able to recite the words of the ritual with undeviating accuracy as often as may be required, which point being reached, nothing further is looked for by the Craft, and rarely, if ever, offered by the Lecturer. For this state of affairs the Grand Lecturers are not to be held responsible; they are appointed to comply with a certain demand, and they do it; but it is to be regretted that public sentiment should have been so viciously educated, and that the formal repetition of set phrases should have come to be considered of such vital importance to Masonry, to the exclusion, in too many instances, of higher and nobler themes—to the making of the paths that lead to the Temple of greater importance than all the glorious arcana within its precincts. Masonry is a science, and as such appeals to men of intelligence and education, and offers a sure reward to the industrious seeker after its hidden mysteries; but such men will not and cannot be hampered by the mere words in which the formulas of initiation shall be communicated or explained, nor will they consent to fritter away precious time in chasing the shadows of verbiage when they can be better employed in pursuit of solid attainments, of which our system offers such an abundance. We have, then, no hesitation in saying that we have seen with sincere regret the special efforts made within a few years to bend the energies of the Craft to the attainment of uniformity in the ritual—a chimera as unsubstantial as the visions of the night ; that, so far from producing the desired end, has but resulted in the estrangement of brethren, in differences among the workmen on different parts of the building, in the intrusion of crude ideas hatched in the brains of unlettered men—always presented, however, as the ancient work ; in short, of making confusion worse confounded, and substituting the exercise of the lips for the legitimate work of the brain. That the Grand Lodge is the lawful custodian of the work, we freely admit, and that it should always endeavor to maintain the essentials of the ritual in the simple quaintness of the fathers, we acknowledge, but we can see in this no reason why a legitimate duty should be made the vehicle of an attempt to force all men to think and see alike, or to assert an equality of intellect where the Great Architect has refused so to make men ; much less can it be made the apology for secret combinations in behalf of particular systems, by the introduction of which it is hoped not only to make individual instructors always use the same identical words, but to reduce the general mind to a certain line, from which it shall never swerve to the right or left by the breadth of a hair. Yet we have witnessed within a few years a combined, systematic, and secret attempt to displace the authority of Grand Lodges in this particular, and substitute one set of words for another; and we have seen, too, that it has given rise to more heart-burnings, ill blood, and unmasonic demonstrations than anything that has been sought to be fixed upon the institution since its introduction into this country. And the men, too, who are most ardent in this work are generally those who scarcely know that Masonry has a history, a philosophy, or a literature; who are innocently unaware that the "work" which secures their admiration and commands their zeal is but one of the variations that have been made from time to time since the days of the great innovator Preston, and those of his imitator and still greater innovator Webb. The original degrees of Masonry have been so buried under the multiplied additions of ritualists, for the last hundred years, that the Masons of the present day—choose what system they will—cannot hope to approach the simplicity of the original. Why, then, devote our time and attention to mere words? Why quarrel about A, B, or C's work, when we know that neither of them is anything more than a new version of an old story, and that not one of them is in truth the true work practised so recently as 1717? Let us rather seek to retain the essential features of the ritual, with less regard for the mere words in which our ideas may be conveyed, or at least without making the power of machine-like repetition the test of Masonic perfection.

From these premises the reader will easily arrive at the conclusion, that a Grand Lecturer should be something more than a ritualist; that he should be able to instruct the brethren not only in the forms and ceremonies of the several degrees, but in the hidden meaning of the symbols; that, having led them through the courts of the Temple, he should be able to put aside the vail that conceals the inner mysteries, and direct their investigations to higher and nobler themes.

When such are the qualifications required of Grand Lecturers, and they prepare themselves accordingly, a brighter day will dawn upon Masonry, and its disciples will have arrived one stage nearer the accomplishment of its mission.

DISTRICT DEPUTY GRAND MASTERS.

The officers who bear this title have been known to the Craft but a short time, the office having been created to supply a want growing out of the vast increase of the society in modern times. They have, therefore, no inherent powers, and only exercise such

functions as may be specially given them by the constitutions of the Grand Lodge for which they act.
They are really Assistant Deputy Grand Masters, but
are distinguished from the real Deputy by the fact,
that while he may exercise the powers of his office
in any part of the jurisdiction, they are limited to the
supervision of a certain number of Lodges called, for
convenience sake, a Masonic district, whence their
title.   Although the powers exercised by them vary
somewhat in different localities, the general idea is,
that they shall visit all the Lodges in their district
at least once in each year, examine their records and
proceedings, collect statistics of their numbers and
progress, and report annually to the Grand Lodge
their standing, and what—if any—legislation is required to promote their welfare and prosperity.

The appointment of these officers is but an extension of the twentieth of the old Regulations, which
requires the "Grand Master, with his Deputy and
Wardens, to go round and visit all the Lodges about
town (at least once) during his Mastership." When
that regulation was adopted, there were not, probably, a dozen Lodges in London, so that the call
upon the Grand Master's time was not onerous ; but
in some of the American jurisdictions, where there
are from two hundred and fifty to five hundred
Lodges, a single visit to each would be a severe tax

upon the Grand Master's time. Moreover, it it quite as necessary to visit Lodges out of cities as those in them, and it was therefore necessary to devise some plan by which that object could be accomplished ; and this, in our judgment, was most happily effected in the creation of the office of District Deputy.

The brethren who accept these offices by no means acquire honor without labor ; on the contrary, the duties required of them demand much time, no small amount of patience, good address, and familiarity with the laws and usages of the society. In some of the country districts, where the Lodges are located at considerable distances from each other, it is often necessary for the Deputy to leave his usual avocations and travel many weary miles, in the discharge of his duty ; and yet, we are proud to say, those duties are rarely neglected. The benefits that thus accrue to Masonry may not be lightly estimated ; and while we should be glad, for the sake of the Craft, to see the system adopted in every Grand Lodge jurisdiction, and trust to see it always continued in our own, we would bespeak a larger appreciation of the officers themselves, and such a recognition of their importance as would enable them to appear in Grand Lodge at the Annual Communications, without expense to them individually. While the Masters and Wardens represent their particular Lodges, the District Deputies represent a number, and are qualified by actual inspection to speak of their condition and needs, and thus enable the Grand Lodge to legislate advisedly on matters that relate to the welfare of the great body of the Craft.

Their immediate value, however, is in the fact of their availability in arranging unseemly bickerings, and preserving that concord and unity so essential to the well-being of Lodges, by counsel, by admonition, and—when needed—by the strong hand of authority. A kind word spoken in season may quench the fires of passion about to break forth, and while the belligerents, from a sense of wounded or mistaken pride, might fail to allow for each other's faults, or take the first step toward reconciliation, the District Deputy could gracefully do so, as one of the duties of his office ; and if these brethren never did anything else, we hold that their appointment would be most commendable.

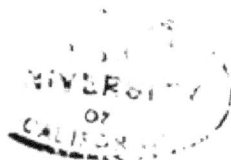

APPENDIX.

———•◦•———

FORM OF PETITION FOR A NEW LODGE.

To the M. W. Grand Master of Masons of the State of ....

THE undersigned petitioners, being Ancient Free and Accepted Master Masons, having the prosperity of the fraternity at heart, and willing to exert their best endeavors to promote and diffuse the genuine principles of Masonry, respectfully represent—That they are desirous of forming a new Lodge in the ...... of .... to be named ...... No. .... They therefore pray for letters of dispensation, to empower them to assemble as a regular Lodge, to discharge the duties of Masonry, in a regular and constitutional manner, according to the original forms of the Order, and the regulations of the Grand Lodge. They have nominated and do recommend Brother A. B. to be the first Master ; Brother C. D. to be the first Senior Warden, and Brother E. F. to be the first Junior Warden, of said Lodge. If the prayer of this petition shall be granted, they promise a strict conformity to the edicts of the Grand Master, and the constitution, laws and regulations of the Grand Lodge.

———————

FORM OF DISPENSATION FOR A NEW LODGE.

To all whom it may concern :

KNOW YE, That we, A. B., Most Worshipful Grand Master of Ancient, Free and Accepted Masons of ......, having received a petition from a constitutional number of brethren, who have been properly vouched for as Master Masons in good standing, setting forth that, having the honor and prosperity of the Craft at heart, they are desirous of establishing a new Lodge at ...... under our masonic jurisdiction, and requesting a Dispensation for the same :

And whereas there appears to us good and sufficient cause **for** granting the prayer of the said petition ; we, by virtue of the powers in us vested by the ancient Constitutions of the Order, do grant this our DISPENSATION, empowering Brother **A. B. to act** as Worshipful Master, **Brother C. D.** to **act as** Senior Warden, and Brother E. **F.** to act as Junior Warden **of a** Lodge **to** be held under our jurisdiction at ...... by the **name** of ......   And we further authorize the said brethren to *Enter, Pass,* and *Raise* Freemasons, **according to** the Ancient Constitutions of the Order, the customs **and usages of the** Craft, and **the** Rules and Regulations **of** the **Most Worshipful Grand** Lodge of ......, and not otherwise.   And **this our DISPENSATION** shall continue of force until the Grand Lodge aforesaid shall grant a Warrant of Constitution for the same, or this DISPENSATION be revoked **by us, or the** authority of the aforesaid Grand Lodge.

[L. S.]

Given under our hand, and the seal of the Grand Lodge, at ...... this .... day of ......, A∴ L∴ 58 .

Q...... R......,

Y...... **Z**......
Grand Secretary.

Grand Master.

FORM OF WARRANT FOR **A** LODGE.

GRAND MASTER.
DEP. G. MASTER.
SEN. G. WARDEN.
JUN. G. WARDEN.

WE, the Grand Lodge **of the Most** Ancient **and Honorable Fra**ternity of Free **and Accepted Masons, of the** State of ...., in Ample Form assembled, according to the Old Constitutions, regularly and solemnly established under the auspices of Prince Edwin, at the city of York, **in Great Britain, in the** year of **Masonry 4926, viz. :**

The Most Worshipful   Grand Master,
The Right Worshipful   Dep. G. Master,
The Right Worshipful   Sen. G. Warden,

do, by these presents, appoint, authorize, and empower our worthy brother .... to be the Master ; our worthy brother .... to be the Senior Warden ; and our worthy brother .... to be the Junior Warden, of a Lodge of Free and Accepted Masons, to be, by virtue hereof, constituted, formed, and held in .... which Lodge shall be distinguished by the name or style of ...... and the said Master and Wardens, and their successors in office, are hereby respectively authorized and directed, by and with the consent and assistance of a majority of the members of the said Lodge, duly to be summoned and present upon such occasions, to elect and install the officers of the said Lodge as vacancies happen, in manner and form as is, or may be, prescribed by the Constitution of this Grand Lodge.

And further, the said Lodge is hereby invested with full power and authority to assemble upon proper and lawful occasions, to make Masons, and to admit members, as also to do and perform all and every such acts and things appertaining to the Craft as have been and ought to be done, for the honor and advantage thereof, conforming in all their proceedings to the Constitution of this Grand Lodge, otherwise this Warrant, and the powers thereby granted, to cease and be of no further effect.

 Given under our hands and the seal of our Grand Lodge, at the city of ......, in the United States of America, this.... day of ......, in the year of our Lord one thousand eight hundred and ......, and in the year of Masonry five thousand eight hundred and ......

       ....

       Grand Secretary.

Registered in the Book of the Grand Lodge,
   Page ....

FORM OF A LODGE CERTIFICATE.

To ALL FREE AND ACCEPTED MASONS ON THE FACE OF THE GLOBE
 —GREETING :

We, the Master and Wardens of ...... Lodge No. ... Free and Accepted Masons, constituted under a charter from the M. W. Grand Lodge of the State of ......, do certify that our worthy brother ...... has been regularly initiated as an Entered Appren-

13

tice, passed to the degree of Fellow Craft, and raised to the sub-
lime degree of Master Mason, and is distinguished for his zeal and
fidelity to the Craft. We do therefore recommend that he be received and acknowledged as such by all true and accepted Freemasons wheresoever dispersed.

In testimony whereof we have granted him this certificate under
our hands and the seal of the Lodge (having first caused our worthy brother to sign his name in the margin), this .... day of ....
A.D. 18.., A. L. 58..

W. M.   S. W.
Sec'y.   J. W.

This is to certify that .... Lodge No. .. is a legally constituted Lodge, working under the jurisdiction of the M. W. Grand
Lodge of ......

       585.

          .... Grand Sec'y.

FORM OF A GRAND LODGE DIPLOMA.

We, the Grand Lodge of the State of New York, by these presents
testify and declare to all whom it may concern, that our brother
........, who has signed his name in the margin hereof, is a regular Master Mason of ...... Lodge No. .., as appears to us by the
certificate of the said Lodge held under our jurisdiction in the
...... county of ...... State of New York, in the United States
of America. In testimony whereof we have caused our seal to be
hereunto affixed, and our Grand Secretary to subscribe the same,
at the city of New York, this .. day of .... A. D. 18.. A. L. 58..

         .... Grand Secretary.

FORM OF A DIMIT.

FREE AND ACCEPTED MASONS.

....   Lodge No. ....
Acknowledging the jurisdiction of the Grand Lodge of the State
of ...., to all whom it may concern, greeting : This certifies

that brother ...., whose name appears in the margin of this dimit, is a Master Mason, and was a member of this Lodge in good standing and clear of the books, and as such we do cordially commend him to the fraternal guard of all true Free and Accepted Masons, wherever dispersed around the globe.

In testimony whereof we have caused this dimit to be signed by the Master, and the seal of the Lodge to be attached, this .... day of ...... A. D. 18.., A. L. 58..

.... Secretary.   .... Master.

FORM OF TRIALS AND APPEALS.

THE first step to be taken toward a Masonic trial is, of course, to prefer charges, or make a complaint. The important requisites of a complaint are, that it should be brief, and yet comprehensive, clearly defining the nature of the offense charged, with an accurate specifying of the time, place and circumstances of its commission. This, when the transaction took place out of the Lodge, may be preferred by any brother, but should properly be presented by the Junior Warden. It may be in this form :

1.—Complaint.

To the W. Master, Wardens and Brethren of Triluminar Lodge, No. 800 : Brother A. B. is hereby charged with *immoral and unmasonic conduct :*

First Specification.—That the said A. B., on the first day of April 1859, in the public street, at Freetown, in the county of ....., was in a state of intoxication from the use of strong and spirituous liquors, in violation of his duty as a Mason, and to the scandal and disgrace of the Masonic Fraternity.

Second Specification.—That the said A. B., on the first day of April, 1859, at Freetown aforesaid, and at various other times and places, in the year 1859, was intoxicated with strong and spirituous liquors, although admonished therefor by the Master and Wardens of this Lodge, in violation of his duty as a Mason, to the great scandal and disgrace of the Fraternity ; and it is hereby demanded, that the said A. B. be dealt with therefor, according to Masonic law and usage.

S. L., *Junior Warden.*

Dated April 9, 1859.

2.—Complaint (in another form.)

To the W. Master, Wardens and Brethren of Triluminar Lodge, No. 800 : Brother C. D. is hereby charged with *immoral and unmasonic conduct* :

First Specification.—That the said C. D., on the first day of April, 1859, at Freetown, in the county of ...., in the presence and hearing of Bro. E. F., and others, spoke and declared of Bro. G. H., of **Anchor** Lodge, **No.** 801, these words in substance : that the said G. H. was a dishonest man ; that he was a knave and a cheat ; and that he was a liar, to the great injury of the said G. H., and to the common scandal and disgrace of the Masonic Fraternity.

Second Specification.—That the said C. D., on the first day of April, 1859, **at Freetown** aforesaid, in the presence and hearing of Mr. Y. Z., and others, publicly spoke and declared of the said G. H., who was not present, that he, the said G. H., was a dishonest man, a knave, a cheat and a liar, in violation of the duties of the said C. D. as a Master Mason, **to the great** injury of the said G. H., and to the common scandal and disgrace of the said Anchor Lodge, No. 801, and of the Masonic Fraternity ; and it is therefore hereby demanded, **that the said C. D. be put upon** trial therefor.

S. L., Junior Warden.

Dated April 9, 1859.

These forms might be **indefinitely** multiplied, but these will be **sufficient to show** the manner and importance of specifying **time, place** and circumstances constituting the offense.

This charge (and that contained in **the first** form will hereafter be followed) having been **presented** in open Lodge, and received, **the Master** thereupon appoints commissioners to hear and try the **same, pursuant to the provisions of** the constitution, which **is entered upon the minutes.** The charges need not be entered, but the nature of them **should be.** It is then **the duty** of the Secretary immediately to serve upon the **accused a** copy **of the charges, with** the following notice annexed :

3.—Notice of Charges.

Bro. **A. B.** : Take notice, that the within (or foregoing) is a copy of the charges preferred against **you, at a stated** communication of **Triluminar Lodge, No. 800, held on the 9th of** April, inst., and

that Bros. R. S., T. U. and V. N. were appointed commissioners
to hear and try the same.

P. Q., *Secretary.*

Dated, April 10, 1859.

Should the commissioners determine, at the time the charges
are preferred (and it is recommended that they should in all cases,
if possible), when and where they will meet for trial, the Secretary
may add to the above notice the following : "and that they will
meet for that purpose on the 20th instant, at 7o'clock P. M., at
Triluminar Lodge room, at Freetown, at or before which time
you are required to answer said charges."

In case the accused absent himself, so that the charges cannot
be personally served, the copy may be transmitted by mail, if his
residence be known ; if not, after a reasonable time, and after diligent inquiry, the Secretary should report the fact to the Lodge
for their further action. In all cases the prosecutor or Secretary
should take care that the accused be served with notice of the time
and place of meeting of the commissioners for trial, at the time of
service of the charges.

The charges being served, it is the first duty of the accused, if
he has an objection to any of the commissioners, to make his chal-
lenge, that the master, if satisfied that there is ground for it,
may supply the vacant place by another appointment. If there
be doubts as to its foundation, the master, or other commissioners, may act as triers ; but it is recommended that if there be reasonable objection, or probable cause therefor be manifest, that the
commissioner challenged remove all question by resignation.

The tribunal being properly constituted, it is next the duty of
the accused to answer the charges. As this must be in every
case equivalent to the well-known plea of "Not Guilty," it is
scarcely necessary to furnish a form, yet, for the sake of making
up a complete record, in cases of appeal, one is subjoined :

4.—Answer.

C. D., in person, denies the charges made against him, and every matter and thing contained in the several specifications of
the same, and demands trial thereon.

Of course this answer will vary according to the facts of each
case. One specification may be admitted and another denied.

The **charge and** specifications may be admitted, and matters set
up **in extenuation or excuse.** Assuming the answer to be a denial
the issued is formed, **and the** parties proceed **to trial.** To procure
the attendance **of witnesses** on **either side, some process** may be
necessary. If the witness be not **a** Mason, his attendance **must,**
of course, be voluntary ; but **a** Mason **is** bound to obey a summons. This may be issued by any master **of a** Lodge (Constitution § 56), and in the following form :

5.—Summons for Witness.

To Bro. I. J. : **You are** hereby summoned **and required** to attend as a **witness before** the commissioners appointed for the trial
of A. B., on certain charges preferred against him, on **the** 20th
day of April, **instant, at 7 o'clock P. M.,** at the Lodge room of Triluminar Lodge, **No. 800, in Freetown,** and there to testify the
truth, according **to your knowledge.**

K. L., *Master.*

Dated, **April 16, 1859.**

This may be made to answer **for several** witnesses, **by inserting
their names and** adding the **words "and** each of **you"** after **the**
word **"**you.**"** The brother disobeying such **a summons** may be
proceeded against as in **case of** disobedience to any **other summons.** For this purpose the **person serving it** should **note upon
it when** and how it is served.

The commissioners, having **met for trial, should organize ; that
is to say,** one of **their** number (and usually **the first named)** should
preside, though they may choose another for **that** purpose ; and
another of them should be **chosen** to act as their clerk, and keep
the minutes **of their proceedings.** A copy of the resolution **under**
which they were appointed, together with their appointment,
should be furnished them **by the Secretary. They** should keep
minutes of their proceedings, which may **be in this** form :

6.—Minutes of Commissioners.

The commissioners appointed for the trial of A. B., on **the**
charges a copy of which is hereto annexed (marked A) pursuant to
the following resolution (copy resolution), **assembled** at the Lodge
room of Triluminar Lodge, No. **800, on Wednesday evening, the**
20th **of April, 1859 :**

Present : R. S., T. U. and V. N., commissioners. R. S. offici-ated as chairman, and V. N. was chosen clerk.

A. B. appeared before them and objected to T. U., one of the commissioners, on the ground that he was present at the meeting of the Lodge when the charges were preferred, and voted for their reference.

Bro. T. U. stated that he had formed no opinion on the subject, and the other commissioners decided that he was competent to act as commissioner, to which Bro. B. took an exception.

The charges were then read by Bro. S. L., Junior Warden, to-gether with the answer of Bro. A. B.

Bro. B. requested that P. S., Esq., an attorney and not a Ma-son, should examine the witnesses on his behalf and assist him in his defense. The commissioners decided against the request, but further decided that he might employ the services of any brother to assist him in defense ; to which Bro. B. took an exception. He then employed Bro. N. O. to assist him as counsel. Bro. O. ob-jected to the form of the charges as being vague and uncertain, but the commissioners decided them to be sufficient ; to which Bro. O. took an exception.

Bro. E. F. was then introduced as a witness by the Junior War-den, and testified as a Master Mason as follows : I am acquainted with Bro. A. B. ; I saw him on Main street, in Freetown, on the first day of April last ; I was on the opposite side of the street ; he appeared to be much intoxicated (objection was made to the *ap-pearance* of accused, but it was overruled and an exception taken) · he was there for about half an hour ; he reeled as he walked, &c.

On cross-examination Bro. E. F. further testified : I know that Bro. B. had been sick, &c.

The commissioners then adjourned to meet at the same place on Thursday evening, the 21st April 1859, at 7 o'clock P. M.

Thursday evening, April 21, 1859.

The commissioners met pursuant to adjournment : present all the commissioners and also Bro. L. the Junior Warden and Bro. A. B. and his counsel Bro. O.

Bro. U. officiated as chairman.

Mr. H. C. was then introduced as a witness by the Junior War-den, and stated as follows :

I was in Freetown on the first day of April instant, &c

The proofs on the part of the complainant here rested.

Bro. O., on behalf of Bro. A. B., then produced the sworn affidavit of Mr. J. B., to which the Junior Warden objected, on the ground that Mr. B. should be produced for cross-examination.

The commissioners sustained the objection on that ground, and Bro. O. took an exception.

Mr. B. was then produced, and the Junior Warden then consented that his affidavit might be read, which was read accordingly, and is hereto annexted (marked **B**).

The Junior Warden then cross-examined Mr. B., who stated as follows, &c.

The proofs being closed, after hearing both parties, the commissioners decided to meet again on the 23d day of April instant, to determine on their report.

Saturday, April 23, 1859.

The commissioners again met by themselves, and after consultation decided upon their report, a copy of which is hereto annexed (marked C), and notified the parties thereof.

Signed by the Commissioners.

These minutes have been given in this extended form because they present a convenient way of stating certain facts and proceedings on trial. Thus, the statement of formal objections and the grounds of them, together with the decision thereon of the commissioners (which should always be stated), are here set forth ; also, that the Junior Warden acted as prosecutor ; that the employment of an attorney not being a Mason was not permitted, but that the accused was permitted to have counsel ; that the first witness testified in his character as a Master Mason, and that the second witness, not being a Mason, made his statement merely, no oath being administered to either ; that the testimony is taken down in the words of the witness, and of course in the first person as he spoke ; that the precise point objected to is stated ; that the time and place of each adjournment are noted ; that a sworn affidavit was not admitted because no opportunity was given for cross-examination ; and, finally, that the commissioners met alone and decided upon their report, and then gave notice to the parties ; all of which may furnish useful hints to those engaged in such trials, without further comment ; it being presumed that the usual forms of such proceedings and the ordinary rules of evidence are understood and will be observed. It is at the option of the commissioners whether they will admit any one to be present but the parties and the witnesses testifying, but on all such occasions none but Masons should be admitted, except the witness not a Mason, and while testifying.

As the form of the notice given to the parties by the commissioners (Constitution, § 57) may be desired, it is here given, and may be as follows.

7.—Notice of Decision.

To Bro. S., Junior Warden, and Bro. A. B. .

You will each take notice that we have agreed upon and signed our report in the matter of charges against Bro. A. B., referred to us, by which we have found the charges sustained, and Brother B. guilty thereof, and that the expenses of the proceedings be paid by him ; and that we shall present the report to Triluminar Lodge at its stated communication, on the 30th April instant.

(Signed by the Commissioners.)

Dated April 23d, 1859.

The trial being concluded and the report thus agreed upon, the commissioners will have it drawn up in form for the action of the Lodge. This report need not, in the first place, contain anything but the facts found and the conclusions arrived at thereon by the commissioners. These conclusions, like those of any other committee, should be in the form of resolutions, for the definite action of the Lodge. Should the Lodge, on the report coming in, desire to hear the testimony read or any of the decisions stated, it will be the duty of the commissioners to comply.

The report may be in the following form :

8.—Report of Commissioners.

To the W. Master, Wardens and Brethren of Triluminar Lodge, No. 800.

The commissioners appointed for the trial of Bro. A. B., on charges of intoxication heretofore preferred in this Lodge, respectfully report :

That they met at the Lodge room of this Lodge on Wednesday evening, the 20th of April last past, and proceeded to hear and try the matters referred to them.

That objections were presented to Bro. U., one of their number, which they overruled, and **also** refused to permit Bro. **B. to appear** by counsel, not being **a Mason,** and thereupon Bro. N. O. appeared for him. That objections **were** made to the charges, which were overruled.

That they proceeded to take testimony (in the course of which they decided not to admit a sworn affidavit), and Bro E. F. and Mr. H. C. and Mr. J. B. were examined as **witnesses.**

That they held three **meetings, the** last of which was **for the purpose of** agreeing upon and preparing their report.

That **from the testimony** before them they **find the** following facts :

1. **That Bro. A. B.** was intoxicated with strong and spirituous liquors, **in a public place,** at Freetown, on the first day of April, 1859.

2. That Bro. A. B. has been at least **twice** intoxicated in a public place, in Freetown aforesaid, within two weeks previous to the said first day of April, 1859.

They therefore recommend the adoption of the following resolutions :

Resolved, That the charges **of intoxication** against Bro. A. B., **made** and presented **to this** Lodge **on** the 9th day of April, 1859, are sustained, and that he is guilty of the said charges.

Resolved, That Bro. A. B. be and he is hereby suspended from this Lodge, **and** from the rights and privileges of Masonry, for the **space** of three months from this date.

The charges and expenses of the commissioners amount to the **sum of three dollars,** which they adjudge that **Bro. A. B.** should **pay, of all which they** have notified the Junior Warden and Bro. **A. B. All of which is** respectfully submitted,

R. S. ⎱
T. U. ⎰ *Commissioners.*
V. W. ⎰

Dated, April 23, 1859.

If the resolutions be adopted, the Secretary of the Lodge should transcribe them on his minutes, together with the adjudication as **to charges and** expenses. The resolutions, **however,** are subject to the action of the Lodge, who may reverse the decision of the commissioners, or, if sustained, may amend the resolution as to the penalty by **increasing or** diminishing it ; the decision of the commissioners, however, as to expenses is final (Cons. § 61.) Should the resolutions be adopted (and for this purpose a majority vote is sufficient, unless the by-laws provide differently,) and the accused be absent from the Lodge, it is the duty of the Secretary to furnish him immediately with a copy of the resolutions and of the award as to expenses, with a notice, which may be in this form :

9.—Notice of Judgment.

To Bro. A. B. :

Take notice, that the foregoing is a copy of resolutions adopted by Triluminar Lodge, No. 800, at their communication held at their Lodge room in Freetown, on the 30th day of April instant, together with a copy of the award made by the commissioners as to expenses.

P. Q. *Secretary.*

Dated, April 30th, 1859.

Thus have been presented the ordinary proceedings from complaint to judgment on a Masonic trial on charges preferred *in a Lodge.* Some of them may be found practically unnecessary, but the complaint, minutes and report are deemed important, and should be substantially followed in every case. Other proceedings, under the title of the Constitution, entitled "Of Trial and Its Incidents," may be adapted to them, varying the allegations to suit the case, and bearing in mind that in all the cases mentioned in section 54 the decision of the commissioners is final, unless an appeal be taken from it. (§ 58.) In these cases the report will be made to the Grand Lodge, and the minutes, with the report annexed, filed in the office of the Grand Secretary, and notice given to the parties by the commissioners. Their report, in such cases, need not conclude with resolutions, but with an award of judgment in the nature of both a verdict and sentence. It may be in this form, in place of the recommendation of resolutions :

10.—Report of Commissioners (*another form*).

The said commissioners do therefore adjudge and determine as follows :

1. That the charges of intoxication against Bro. A. B., of Triluminar Lodge, No. 800, preferred by Bro. C. D., of Anchor Lodge, No. 801, on the 9th day of April, 1859, are sustained, and that he is guilty of the said charges.

APPENDIX.

2. That the said Bro. A. B. be and he is hereby suspended from said Triluminar Lodge, and from the rights and privileges of Masonry, for the space of three months from this date.

3. That the said A. B. be adjudged to pay the charges and expenses of the proceedings on this trial.

The charges and expenses, &c., (as in the preceding report, except as to parties notified, and add) and our report has been duly filed with the R. W. Grand Secretary (dated and signed by the commissioners).

The following may be the form of their notice :

11.—Notice of Judgment by Commissioners.

To ...... and .. ... :

Take notice that we have this day made and signed our report to the Grand Lodge, by which we have adjudged and determined that Bro. A. B. is guilty of the charges preferred against him, and that he is suspended from Triluminar Lodge, No. 800, and from the rights and privileges of Masonry, for the space of three months, and that he do pay the costs and expenses of the proceedings before us, amounting to the sum of three dollars.

Signed by the Commissioners.

Dated, April 23, 1859.

The subject of Appeals next claims our attention, and we shall still follow the form of proceedings after trial on charges preferred in a Lodge against a member.

The time limited in every case for bringing an appeal is six months (§ 58) ; but where a party is intending to appeal it is advisable that he give notice of it immediately, which may be in the following form :

12.—Notice of Appeal.

To P. Q., Secretary of Triluminar Lodge, No. 800 :

Take notice, that I shall bring an appeal from the action of said Lodge on the 30th day of April, 1859, in passing sentence of suspension on me for three months, to the M. W. Grand Lodge of the State of New York (or the M. W. Grand Master, R. W. Deputy Grand Master, or R. W. District Deputy Grand Master of this district, as he may choose,) on the grounds to be stated in my appeal.

Dated, May 4, 1859.   A. B.

On receiving this notice, the Secretary of the Lodge—or, in all cases not under section 60, the commissioners—will transmit to the Grand Lodge, or Grand officer, as the case may be, a copy of the minutes of proceedings embracing the evidence, with a copy of the report, to the Lodge—marked C and numbered 8—annexed, all duly attested and certified ; and by carefully observing these directions it may always be done promptly. This, if filed with the Grand Secretary, may be furnished to the Grand Lodge, or its Committee on Appeals, or to the Grand officer appealed to, when desired. When the appeal is to a Grand officer, the report may be transmitted to him directly, to be by him afterwards filed with the Grand Secretary. The appellant should next prepare his appeal, which may be in this form :

13.—Appeal.

To the M. W. Grand Lodge of the State of New York (or M. W. Grand Master) :

The undersigned hereby appeals to you from the decision of Triluminar Lodge, No. 800, made April 30, 1859, in passing sentence of suspension on him for three months, and he specifies the following as the ground of his appeal :

1. That F. U., one of the commissioners on his trial, was incompetent to act, having been present at the meeting of said Lodge when the charges were preferred, and voted for their reference.

2. That the commissioners erred in deciding that P. S., Esq., should not be allowed to assist the undersigned in his defense.

3. That the second specification of the charges is vague and uncertain.

4. That the commissioners erred in receiving testimony as to appearances of intoxication.

5. That they erred in rejecting the sworn affidavit of J. R.

6. That the proofs in the case were not sufficient to warrant the finding of the commissioners.

7. That the Lodge erred in passing the resolution of suspension by a majority vote.

All of which appears by the papers, proceedings and evidence in the case.

Dated, May 11, 1859.   A. B.

A copy of this appeal should be served on the Secretary of the

Lodge ; and it is best, also, to serve a copy on the appellate tribunal or officer. **Within ten** days (this is suggested as an admirable time, there being no regulation on the subject,) an answer should **be made to the** appeal by the Lodge. As in most cases this is **merely taking issue,** the form of an answer on appeal may be unnecessary ; yet one is subjoined, as follows :

14.—Answer to Appeal.

Triluminar Lodge, No. 800, answers **the appeal of A. B. and says :**

That the said Lodge denies that there **is** any error **in** the proceedings of said Lodge, **or** of the commissioners appointed for the trial of the said A. B., **and further** says **that the** decision **of said Lodge in said case is sustained** both by the **law** and **evidence therein applicable thereto.**

Dated, May 21, 1859.   S. L., *Junior Warden.*

This is **very general, and if a specific denial is deemed necessary** —taking issue **upon each of the grounds of** appeal and assigning reasons therefor—it may be made after **the** foregoing form in commencement, and adding thereto **as follows :**

Because the said Lodge **says as to** the first ground **of appeal, &c.**

And because the said Lodge says as to the second ground of appeal, &c.

The case being thus fairly brought up on appeal, the Grand **Lodge** or Grand officer may hear **the** same, either **by** oral argument, **or** the appeal and answer thereto may be **made** sufficiently **full** to call attention to all the **points in the case and** the reasons **therefor. If the** Secretary of the Lodge shall **have omitted a transcript of the proceedings of** the Lodge, and the same be required to make **the case perfectly understood, the Grand Master, Deputy** Grand Master, or District Deputy Grand Master may make an order in this form :

15.—Order on Appeal.

OFFICE OF THE GRAND MASTER OF MASONS, }
May 28, 18.. }

To the W. Master, Warden and Brethren **of Triluminar Lodge,** No. 800 :

Bro. A. B. having duly appealed **from the** decision **of your** Lodge made on the 30th April, 1859, **suspending him** for three months, you are hereby required to transmit, by the hand of your Secretary and seal of your Lodge, a transcript of all the proceedings of your Lodge, in the case of the said A. B., from the time of the presentation of the charges against him until the final action of your Lodge thereon, with the several dates thereof, together with all papers and documents relating thereto not heretofore returned, within .... days from the receipt of this order by you.

Given under my hand and private seal on the day and year first above written.

...., *Grand Master.*

After argument the appellate tribunal will, with all convenient dispatch, pronounce the decision. If made by a Grand officer, it should be filed, together with the appeal papers, in the office of the Grand Secretary, and may be in this form :

16.—Decision on Appeal.

OFFICE OF THE GRAND MASTER OF MASONS, &c., June 4, 1859.

IN THE MATTER OF THE APPEAL
OF
BROTHER A. B.

Brother A. B. having appealed from the decision of Triluminar Lodge, No. 800, made on the 30th day of April, 1859, by which he was suspended from the rights and privileges of Masonry for three months, on charges of intoxication ; and having heard the case, I have carefully considered the facts appearing on said appeal, and the grounds of error alleged by him. There does not seem to be any error or irregularity in the proceedings, or in the several decisions of the commissioners on the trial, and the facts of the case warrant the conclusions of the commissioners and the decision of the Lodge.

[If the officers desire to review the facts or comment upon any of the points taken, he may here insert his remarks and reasons.]

My judgment and decision, therefore, is, that the proceedings and decisions of Triluminar Lodge, No. 800, in the case of Bro. A. B., be and the same are hereby affirmed.

...., *Grand Master.*

If the decision be reversed, the appellate officer will vary the second paragraph and give his reasons for dissenting from the conclusions of the commissioners and Lodge, and use the word "reversed" in the last paragraph, instead of "affirmed." Should he desire to make any special order in the case, it may be added at the end.

When an appeal is taken from the decision of a Grand officer, on appeal to the Grand Lodge the case will be heard on the papers which were before him, and it will only need the following and final form of an appeal to bring up the matter, which should be served on the Lodge through its proper officer, a reasonable time (say twenty days) before the annual communication of the Grand Lodge, and a copy transmitted to the Grand Secretary forthwith.

17.—Final Appeal to Grand Lodge.

To the M. W. Grand Master (or R. W. Deputy Grand Master) and the W. Master Wardens and Brethren of Triluminar Lodge, No. 800 :

The undersigned, A. B., hereby appeals to the M. W. Grand Lodge of the State of New York, from the decision of the M. W. Grand Master, made in and by his order of June 4th, 1859, in the case of this appellant, affirming the decision of said Lodge on the 30th April, 1859, in the same case, on the grounds particularly stated and set forth in his appeal to the M. W. Grand Master, dated May 11, 1859, and respectfully prays your consideration thereof and judgment thereon.

Dated, June 6, 1859.   A. B.

In the nature of the case, no answer to this appeal is required ; and when the appeal comes before the Grand Lodge it will take the direction prescribed by its rules and usages.

From the foregoing general forms and directions, sufficient may be gathered to apply to every case of Masonic discipline and trial, between any parties and whatever may be the decision. To have extended the forms, or adapted those given to every varying change, would be great labor without adequate benefit, and especially in the great variety of charges. It should be remarked that, when the charges are based upon a section of the constitution, or of the Lodge by-laws, it should be plainly and distinctly referred to.

Should the accused admit the charges when served upon him, proof of such admission or confession will be all that the commissioners are required to have made, and they will make up their minutes and report accordingly, adapting the foregoing forms.

If the accused fails to appear and answer the charges after personal service, the commissioners may proceed, after taking proof of such service, to take proof of the charges, and in such case the Master should appoint some brother to appear for him. The minutes and report in such cases should be full, and the forms given can readily be modified to suit such a state of facts.

STANDARD FORM OF BY-LAWS.

[Intended to serve as a guide in the formation of by-laws for Subordinate Lodges, and subject to such alterations, not inconsistent with the Constitution, as the convenience of the Lodges may dictate.]

ARTICLE I.

§ 1. The stated meetings of this Lodge shall be on the .. and .. days in every month. The hour of meeting, from April 1 to October 1, shall be 8 o'clock, and 7½ o'clock the remainder of the year.

§ 2. Special meetings may be called by the Master, upon any emergency which he, in his judgment, may deem necessary ; but no business shall be transacted by such special meeting but that for which it was called.

ARTICLE II.

§ 3. The members of this Lodge are all who have been or may be initiated in or affiliated therewith, who have subscribed their names to these by-laws, and who have not withdrawn or been excluded for unmasonic conduct or non-payment of dues. (See sections 24 to 27, and sections 85 and 88, Constitution.)

ARTICLE III.

OFFICERS—THEIR ELECTION, INSTALLATION, AND DUTIES.

§ 4. The officers of this Lodge shall be ranked and entitled as follows :

      1. THE MASTER.
      2. THE SENIOR WARDEN.
      3. THE JUNIOR WARDEN.

4. THE TREASURER.
5. THE SECRETARY.
6. THE SENIOR DEACON.
7. THE JUNIOR DEACON.
8. THE STEWARDS, OR MASTERS OF CEREMONIES.
9. THE TYLER.

the officers shall be elected at the stated communication next preceding the festival of St. John the Evangelist, and be installed on or before the next stated meeting thereafter.

§ 6. Any member .... months in arrears for dues, shall not be entitled to vote at said election.

§ 7. The duties of the officers of this Lodge, in addition to those not proper to be written, are as follows :

THE MASTER.

To preserve the Warrant of the Lodge with unfailing care, and deliver it to his successor in office ; to see that these by-laws, the Constitution of the Grand Lodge of the State of New York, and the Ancient Constitutions of Freemasonry, be duly understood, respected, and obeyed by the members ; to represent the Lodge, in conjunction with the Senior and Junior Wardens, at all the **Grand** communications of the M. W. Grand Lodge ; to draw all orders on the Treasurer, with the consent and approbation of the Lodge ; to see that all cases of offense against the laws of the Order be fairly dealt with, according to these by-laws, and the constitutions and rules of Masonry ; to report to the Lodge his proceedings in the Grand Lodge, and to cause the printed transactions to be read for the information of the brethren.

THE SENIOR WARDEN.

In addition to those duties which appertain to every individual Mason, the duties of the Senior Warden are : to succeed to and exercise all the powers of the Master in the event of his absence ; to represent the Lodge, in conjunction with the Master and Junior Warden, in the Grand Lodge ; to aid the Master in governing the Craft during the hours of labor.

THE JUNIOR WARDEN.

It is the duty of the Junior Warden to exercise all the powers of he Master, in the absence of the two officers above him ; to represent the Lodge, in conjunction with the Master and Senior Warden, in the Grand Lodge ; to take charge of the Craft during the hours of refreshment.

THE TREASURER

Is to receive all moneys from the hands of the Secretary ; pay out the same by order of the Master and consent of the Lodge ; to submit his accounts, when required by the Master or Lodge, for examination ; to deliver to his successor in office all the moneys, books, vouchers, and other properties of the Lodge he may have in his possession.

THE SECRETARY.

The duty of this officer is to record the proceedings of the Lodge ; to receive all moneys due the Lodge and pay the same to the Treasurer ; to prepare the usual Returns to the Grand Lodge, in proper time and in accordance with the Constitution, and forward the same to the Grand Secretary ; to deliver up to his successor in office all the books, seal, and other property of the Lodge.

THE SENIOR DEACON

Is to take part in the active duties of the Lodge ; to be courteous to and provide accommodations for visiting brethren, and act as the proxy of the Master.

THE JUNIOR DEACON

Has especial charge of the door, acts as the proxy of the Senior Warden, and attends to such other duties as are pointed out to him by the Master or Senior Warden, in accordance with the usages of Masonry and the by-laws of his Lodge.

THE STEWARDS

Are to assist in the preparation of candidates, and to assist the Senior Deacon in the discharge of his duties.

THE TYLER.

The duties of the Tyler are : to tile the Lodge under the direct orders of the Master ; to serve notices, summons, etc., issued under the authority of the Master and the Lodge ; and for the faithful performance of these duties he shall receive .... dollars per year for his services.

OTHER OFFICERS.

The Lodge may, in its discretion, appoint a Chaplain, a Marshal, and an Organist, whose duties shall correspond with their titles.

ARTICLE IV.

TRUSTEES—THEIR ELECTION AND DUTIES.

§ 8. There shall be chosen by ballot, at the annual election, three Trustees, who shall hold in trust for the Lodge all stocks, securities, investments, and funds in deposit or interest, and shall have power to transfer, exchange, or deposit the same, or any part thereof, whenever required by a vote of the Lodge ; deposits to be made in such institution as may be directed by the Lodge, and no amount shall be drawn from such deposit without the order of the Lodge.

§ 9. In case of a vacancy in the office of Trustee, the Lodge may at any time proceed to fill the same, after two weeks' notice.

ARTICLE V.

MEMBERSHIP—HOW ACQUIRED.

§ 10. Any person desirous of being initiated in this Lodge must be proposed in writing by a member thereof, at a stated communication. The member making the proposition shall state therein the age, birthplace, profession, and residence of the person proposed. If the Lodge consents to receive the proposition, it shall be referred to a special committee of three, whose duty it shall be to make a thorough investigation into the physical, mental, and moral qualification of said candidate, and make their report thereof at the next stated meeting thereafter, unless further time be granted. On the report of said committee being made, the Lodge shall proceed to ballot for the candidate, and, if no black ball appear against him, he shall be declared elected ; but should one black ball appear against him, he shall be rejected.

§ 11. No person can receive any degree in this Lodge, or become a member thereof, who is not of mature age, sound in mind, perfect in body and limbs, possessing a good character, a trade or profession, or some visible way of acquiring an honest and respectable livelihood, and publicly acknowledging a belief in the existence of a Supreme Being.

§ 12. Any Mason desirous of becoming a member of this Lodge by affiliation, must produce a certificate of having paid his dues in his former Lodge, and of his having left the same in good standing, subject to the conditions set forth in section 10.

ARTICLE VI.

FEES AND DUES.

§ 13. The initiation fee shall be ...... dollars (not less than fifteen.) The affiliation fee .... dollars.

§ 14. The annual dues shall be ..... dollars, payable quarterly.

§ 15. Any member of the Lodge neglecting or refusing to pay his dues for one year, may be stricken from the roll thereof by a vote of the Lodge, at a stated meeting.

§ 16. No person withdrawing from this Lodge can again become a member without being proposed and balloted for anew, subject to the provisions of sections 10 and 13.

§ 17. No member whose name has been stricken from the roll can again become a member of this Lodge without paying up his indebtedness and being proposed and balloted for as in the case of adjoining members.

§ 18. No brother of this Lodge shall be suspended or expelled from membership unless charges be preferred duly specifying his offense, presented by a brother in good standing, and the accused being allowed full opportunity to make his defense.

§ 19. Any brother desirous of withdrawing from this Lodge must pay his indebtedness, and obtain its consent thereto.

ARTICLE VII.

COMMITTEES.

§ 20. The Master, on the night of his installation, shall appoint a committee of three members to be called the Standing Committee, whose duty it shall be to examine the books, vouchers, etc., of the Treasurer and Secretary, from time to time, and to make a detailed report in writing, whenever required. Likewise, to examine and audit all bills, accounts, and claims that may be presented to the Lodge for payment, and report upon the same in writing. Nor shall any account be allowed by the Lodge until it shall have been examined and reported upon by the Standing Committee.

§ 21. When in session, the Lodge may **refer** applications for charity to a Special Committee ; but during the interval the Master and Wardens **shall be a Committee of** Charity, and shall have **power at** any time to draw upon the Treasurer, through the Master, **for a sum** not exceeding five dollars at **one time, to bestow upon a** distressed worthy Master Mason, his wife, widow, **or** orphan child.

§ 22. **Special Committees may be** appointed upon **any** item of **business,** and may consist of as may members as the **Lodge,** in its discretion, may think **proper.** All committees shall **report** at the next stated meeting subsequent to their appointment, and **in** writing, **unless otherwise** ordered by the Lodge. **All committees** shall **be appointed by the Master.** Members who are appointed **to serve** upon committees shall feel bound in honor to give patient and diligent attention to the business of their appointment, and report their conclusions to the Lodge without fear **or favor.**

ARTICLE VIII.

DISCIPLINE, OFFENSES, TRIALS, ETC.

§ 23. **An offense in Masonry is defined to be an act which contravenes these** by-laws, any constitutional rule or edict **of the** Grand Lodge, any requisition of the unwritten law of Masonry, any law of the land, or any law of **God.**

§ 24. **When an** offense **shall be committed by** a member **or** members **of this Lodge against the laws of Freemasonry, and** charges are **preferred thereon, it shall be the duty of the Master to** appoint **not less than three, nor more than seven, disinterested** members of the Lodge, commissioners, **who shall** appoint **a time and** place for the trial, most convenient for those interested, **and** summon the parties and their witnesses. After due investigation of all the facts of the case, the commissioners shall found their **judgment thereon,** and give notice to the parties interested. **A** majority must concur in such judgment, and their judgment, it approved by the Lodge, shall be final, unless an appeal be taken therefrom to the Grand Lodge within six months, in which case it shall be the duty of the commissions, upon receiving notice of such appeal, to transmit their report to the Grand Secretary.

ARTICLE IX.

§ 25. Any portion or the whole of these by-laws may be amended, or others substituted in their stead, at the will of the Lodge, provided the general principles of Freemasonry and the constitutional rules and edicts of the Grand Lodge are carefully maintained. But all amendments, substitutions, etc., must be proposed in writing, read before the Lodge, and laid over for two weeks before a vote of the Lodge is taken, and a vote of two-thirds of the members present shall be necessary to the adoption of such proposition.

Any action or edict of the Grand Lodge altering these by-laws, has the effect of an amendment, without any action on the part of the Lodge.

FORM OF A PROXY.

The Proxy of the Subordinate Lodges should be in the following form, viz :

At a meeting of ...... Lodge, No. ...., held at ...., in the county of ......, in the State of ...., on the ... day of ... A. L. 58..

Resolved, That our Worshipful Brother ......, Past Master (or Master, as the case may be,) of ...... Lodge, No. ..., be and he is hereby appointed Proxy, to represent this Lodge in the Grand Lodge of the State of ...., and he is fully empowered to act in our behalf, in all the transactions of the Grand Lodge, as effectually as if we ourselves were personally present.

All which we have caused to be certified by our Master and Wardens, and the seal of our Lodge to be affixed.

[L. S.]

...., Master.

...., Senior Warden.

...., Junior Warden.

...., Secretary.

CERTIFICATE OF ELECTION.

The certificate of the election of officers in a Subordinate Lodge should be in the following form, and said officers cannot be recognized as members of the Grand Lodge until a proper certificate of election is filed in the Grand Secretary's office :

Be it known, that on the ...... day of .... A. L. 58.., at a regular meeting of .... Lodge, No. .. held in the ......, county of ..... in the State of ...., our worthy Brother ...... was elected Master ; our worthy Brother ...... Senior Warden, and our worthy Brother ...... Junior Warden of the said Lodge, for the ensuing year, and that said Master and Wardens have been duly installed.

In testimony whereof we, the members of the said Lodge, have caused the seal thereof to be hereunto affixed, and our Secretary to sign the same.

[L. s.] .... Secretary.

INDEX.

POPULAR WORKS ON FREEMASONRY

PUBLISHED BY THE

MASONIC PUBLISHING AND MANUFACTURING CO.

432 BROOME STREET, N. Y.

☞ Any book in this list sent by mail to any address in the United States, free of postage, on receipt of the price.

A CYCLOPEDIA OF FREEMASONRY; containing Definitions of the Technical Terms used by the Fraternity. With an account of the rise and progress of Freemasonry and its Kindred Associations—ancient and modern: embracing OLIVER'S DICTIONARY OF SYMBOLICAL MASONRY. Edited by ROBERT MACOY, 33d. *Illustrated with numerous Engravings.* Cloth, gilt side, ...$4 00

GUIDE TO THE ROYAL ARCH CHAPTER; a complete Monitor for Royal Arch Masonry. With full instructions in the degrees of Mark Master, Past Master, Most Excellent Master, and Royal Arch, according to the text of the Manual of the Chapter. By JOHN SHEVILLE, P. G. H. P., of New Jersey, and JAS. L. GOULD, D. G. H. P., of Connecticut. Together with a Historical Introduction, Explanatory Notes, and Critical Emendations. To which are added Monitorial Instructions in the Holy Order of High-Priesthood in Royal Arch Masonry, with the Ceremonies of the Order. By JAS. L. GOULD, M. A., 33d. Cloth—gilt back and side.. 1 50

THE MASONIC HARMONIA; a Collection of Music, Original and Selected, for the use of the Masonic Fraternity. By HENRY STEPHEN CUTLER, Doctor in Music, Director of the Cecilian Choir, etc. Published under the auspices of St. Cecile Lodge, No. 568, City of New York. Half-bound—cloth sides, $1 00..........per doz.10 00

THE GENERAL AHIMAN REZON AND FREEMASON'S GUIDE, containing Monitorial Instructions in the Degrees of Entered Apprentice, Fellow-Craft, and Master Mason, with Explanatory Notes, Emendations, and Lectures: together with the Ceremonies of Consecration and Dedication of New Lodges, Installation of Grand and Subordinate Officers, Laying Foundation Stones, Dedication of Masonic Halls, Grand Visitations, Burial Services, Regulations for Processions, Masonic Calendar, etc. To which are added a RITUAL for a LODGE OF SORROW and the Ceremonies of Consecrating Masonic Cemeteries; also an Appendix, with the Forms of Masonic Documents, Masonic Trials, etc. By DANIEL SICKELS, 33d. Embellished with nearly 300 Engravings and Portrait of the Author.
Bound in fine Cloth—extra—large 12mo.................................... 2 00
" " Morocco, full gilt, for the W. Master's table, with appropriate insignia of the East.... .... 3 50

THE HISTORICAL LANDMARKS and other Evidences of Freemasonry, explained in a series of Practical Lectures, with copious Notes. By GEORGE OLIVER, D. D. 2 vols. Large duodecimo—with Portrait of the Author. Cloth, $5 00. Half Morocco................. 7 00

WASHINGTON AND HIS MASONIC COMPEERS. By SIDNEY HAYDEN, Past Master of Rural Amity Lodge, No. 70, Pennsylvania. Illustrated with a copy of a Masonic Portrait of Washington, *painted from life*, never before published, and numerous other engravings. Cloth—Uniform Style, $2 50. Cloth—full gilt—gilt edges, $3 50. Morocco—full gilt.. 5 00

THE BOOK OF THE ANCIENT AND ACCEPTED SCOTTISH RITE OF FREEMASONRY: containing Instructions in all the Degrees from the Third to the Thirty-third and Last Degree of the Rite, together with Ceremonies of Inauguration, Institution, Installation, Grand Visitations, Refections, Lodges of Sorrow, Adoption, Constitutions, General Regulations, Calendar, etc. By CHARLES T. McCLENACHAN, 33°. *Embellished with upwards of 300 finely-executed engravings, nearly all of which are from original designs.* Cloth, gilt, $5 00

MASONIC LAW AND PRACTICE, WITH FORMS. By LUKE A. LOCKWOOD, Past Grand High-Priest of Connecticut.................... 1 00
DES FREIMAURER'S HANDBUCH (*German*)............................ 75
MORAL DESIGN OF FREEMASONRY. By S. LAWRENCE................. 1 00
BOOK OF THE CHAPTER. By A. G. MACKEY, M. D..................... 1 75
MASONIC VOCAL MANUAL. By ROBERT MACOY..............per doz. 3 00
MANUAL DE LA MASONERIA (*Spanish*). By A. CASSARD........... 10 00
HISTORY OF THE ANCIENT AND ACCEPTED RITE. By ROBT. B. FOLGER. 6 00
LEXICON OF FREEMASONRY. By A. G. MACKEY.......................... 3 00
MASONIC JURISPRUDENCE. By A. G. MACKEY.......................... 2 00
POCKET LIBRARY AND WORKING MONITOR. By CHASE.............. 1 50
MANUAL OF THE LODGE. By A. G. MACKEY............................ 1 75
FREEMASON'S MANUAL. By K. J. STEWART 1 50
MASONIC TRESTLE-BOARD. By C. W. MOORE......................... 1 75
KEYSTONE OF THE MASONIC ARCH. By CHARLES SCOTT.............. 1 25
MASTER WORKMAN. By JOHN K. HALL........................Tuck, 75
MASONIC HARP. By GEORGE W. CHASE............................... 1 00
JURYMAN MASON. By an ENGLISH RECTOR............................ 25
OUTLINES OF SPECULATIVE FREEMASONRY. By TOWN.............. 20
MASON IN HIGH PLACES. By an ENGLISH RECTOR...................... 20

Printed Blank Books for Lodge, Chapter, or Commandery.

LODGE OR CHAPTER REGISTER............................ ....each, 2 50
RECEIPT BOOKS FOR LODGE OR CHAPTER........................... " 3 50
PROPOSITION BOOKS " .... " 4 00
DRAFT BOOKS FOR LODGE OR CHAPTERS .... " 3 50
VISITORS' BOOK 3 50
BLACK BOOK........ .... 3 50
ODE CARDS FOR THE LODGE...............................per dozen, 1 50
ODE CARDS FOR THE CHAPTER......................... " 1 50
PETITIONS FOR MEMBERSHIP...............................per 100, 1 25
LEDGERS AND MINUTE-BOOKS. LARGE AND SMALL BIBLES.
MASONIC LEDGERS—*a new article*........................per quire, 2 50
SECRETARY'S RECEIPTS 3 50
BOOK OF MARKS FOR CHAPTERS.... .... 4 00
QUESTION BOOKS FOR COMMANDERY........... .... 4 00

GOODS OF ALL KINDS FOR

LODGE, CHAPTER, COMMANDERY, ETC.,

ON HAND AND MADE TO ORDER.